THE GEORGE BRETT STORY

THE GEORGE BRETT STORY

John Garrity

Coward, McCann & Geoghegan
New York

Library of Congress Cataloging in Publication Data

Garrity, John.
    The George Brett story.

    1. Brett, George. 2. Baseball players—United States
—Biography. 3. Kansas City Royals (baseball team)
I. Title.
GV865.B715G37   796.357′092′4   [B]   81-9987
ISBN 0-698-11094-3   AACR2

Printed in the United States of America

Portions of this book have appeared in different form in *Sports Illustrated, Sport* magazine, *Baseball Magazine, Popular Sports,* and *City* magazine.

For Pat

Contents

PART ONE

"I NEVER THOUGHT
I'D BE THIS GOOD"

1. Four-zero-zero

"That's as hard as anybody's ever cheered for me,"
John Wathan said, with a wry grin.

It was a Sunday afternoon, August 17, 1980, and the
Kansas City Royals had just beaten the Toronto Blue
Jays, 8-3, in an easy and insignificant ball game. A few
reporters stood around Wathan's cubicle in the clubhouse, asking him to relive his moment of drama in the
Royals eighth inning, when he had strode to the plate
with two out and two on and the Royals ahead, 4-2.

"I kinda looked back as I was going to the plate,"
Wathan, the Royals catcher, told the frantically scrib-
bling audience, "and the guys had their fists clenched
and were yelling, 'Come on, let's go. You've got to get on
base.'" The fans in Royals Stadium had seemed buoy-
antly agitated, noisier and more restless than the situation seemed to dictate. When the pitcher, working

13

from the stretch, fired his first pitch, a ball, a collective murmur swept the stands. The pitcher threw again, ball *two,* and the crowd roared with approval. "I figured there's no way he's gonna walk me," Wathan said. The Duke (as Wathan is called, for his masculine jaw and punch-drunk John Wayne impression) had looked down to the third-base coach, Gordy MacKenzie, for the sign and then stepped back into the box. He swept his bat slowly through the hitting zone a couple of times, staring gravely out at the mound, waiting for the next delivery. But the third pitch, a fast ball, was low and inside. "He didn't even come close," Wathan said. "I was very surprised." The crowd had erupted. Scattered fans jumped to their feet, and a prolonged and excited buzz coursed through the stands as Wathan repeated his sign-reading ritual with MacKenzie. He stepped back in, the crowd beginning to roar. The pitcher had tried to work through the tumult, glaring back over his shoulder at the Royals shortstop U. L. Washington, dancing off second base, with a toothpick dangling from his mouth, and then over at the more relaxed center fielder Amos Otis, taking a short lead off first. Finally, the pitcher raised his leg, heaved his body into the effort, and fired home.

Ball four.

The roar had been deafening. Wathan flipped aside his bat and trotted down to first base, moving the runners up. His other teammates jumped up and down on the dugout steps, screaming and waving their arms. "It was close to a standing ovation," Wathan recalled.

If Wathan did not seem exactly teary-eyed over this unprecedented tribute, it was because he knew the cheers had not really been for him. He had merely set the stage for the man waiting nonchalantly in the on-deck circle—one cheek bulging with chewing tobacco—practicing his swing. The man who, it just happened, had gone 3-for-3 that afternoon to lift his batting average to—was it a misprint on the scoreboard?—.399.

Four-zero-zero. Physicists use the expression, "quantum jump" to describe the discreet properties, sometimes the gross changes, molecular systems owed to minuscule differences in energy levels: furniture dealers recognize the same phenomenon when they price dining room sets at $899.99. Baseball players, too, know that while the difference between .298 and .299 is one point, the difference between .299 and .300 is a lifetime license to brag and about twenty thousand dollars in annual salary. The difference between .399 and .400? Immeasurable. It hadn't been achieved since 1941, when Ted Williams, the "Splendid Splinter," had sealed the books on the era of .400 hitters.

"We were all pulling for him and screaming," Royals outfielder Clint Hurdle said, recalling how George Brett had settled into the box against Blue Jays reliever Mike Barlow. Barlow had struck Brett out the night before, and it was on Brett's mind. "When I got to .399," he admitted afterward, "I said, 'If I hadn't chased a bad ball last night off of Barlow, I probably would be at .400 right now.'"

Barlow had gone to work, trying to shrug off the swelling crowd noise. "He's got a good sinker," Brett said. "I told myself, 'Don't swing at the low ball.'" Barlow's first pitch, a fast ball, cut the plate for a strike.

The tumult lessened instantly, as if a hand on a radio dial turned down the volume. Barlow's second pitch was a sinker, low and away, and the clamor increased again. His next was another sinker, low and in; Brett fouled it off despite his mental vow not to swing at any low balls. The count stood at 1-and-2, the pitcher's advantage.

Brett smiled sheepishly. "I stepped out and said to myself, Jesus, what are you doing? Wait for a pitch you can handle. Try to *drive* it. Hit it hard. I didn't want to hit a tapper back to the pitcher. I didn't want to let those thirty thousand people down."

Brett dug himself back into the box, stared intently at Barlow, and stroked the bat once or twice through the strike zone. Then he drew back, poised, with his weight mostly on his back foot. Barlow heaved himself into the climactic pitch.

Crack! Brett lashed the ball to the opposite field, a hard liner to left that momentarily looked catchable because it was headed for left fielder Garth Iorg. "Usually I just hit the ball and run to first," Brett told reporters afterward, "but I think I was peeking a little bit to see if he was going to catch it or not." Iorg might have; but he read the ball uncertainly, taking a quick step toward the infield—and in that instant he was lost. The ball sailed over his desperately outstretched glove as he scrambled backward. The ball hit just short of the warning track and bounced off the left-field wall, Iorg in pursuit, as Washington, Otis, and Wathan raced around the bases for the delirious, dancing fans, and Brett roared into second with a three-run double. Sirens howled, lights flashed on the scoreboard, the water spectacular spumed and hurled jets of water high into the air, and Brett, with one foot planted on second—in a moment of boyish, spontaneous exultation—took off his batting helmet and thrust his arms into the air for the cheering crowd. "There was almost a mystic quality about it," a close friend remembers. "The bases were cleared and George was left standing alone at center stage." Looming above him, twelve stories tall and forty feet wide, the great crown-topped scoreboard flashed the tantalizing number: *.401*.

"Everything I do is overshadowed by one thing," George Brett said six weeks later, *"four-zero-zero."*

He was annoyed. He had just poled a witching-hour three-run homer in the fourteenth inning to beat the Seattle Mariners, but the reporters who crowded around his locker weren't interested in that. They wanted to know if, with only five games remaining in the 1980 season, he thought he could still hit .400. "Nobody talks about my home runs or RBIs," Brett said petulantly. "If I don't get .400, I'll feel I *failed*. That's all that's been written about. That's all I talk about."

A reporter looked up from his notebook. "Did you know that you broke the Royals RBI record for a season tonight?"

Brett looked surprised. And pleased. "No, I didn't." He threw his T-shirt in the locker. "But see, that's what I mean."

There was a long pause while nobody spoke. Then Brett began to think out loud: "Two points," he murmured, referring to the jump of his average from .385—its lowest level since mid-August—to .387. "If I can get two points a day for five more days, I'll hit .397 . . . and if I have one *great* day . . ." He continued to undress, smiling now. "But I'm not gonna think about it."

Some of the writers smirked. Not think about it? In a sport obsessed with statistics, Brett stood out as a numerologist. If he had been a banker (which he was, in a public-relations capacity), he would have been bent over a calculator figuring interest rates. His recall was digital. He could tell you his average at all the significant points in his career. "I was hitting .291, with three games left in the season when they fired Charley," he would say, recalling the first time the Royals sacked his hitting teacher, Charley Lau, in 1974. Or he would invoke a long-forgotten slump, saying, "On May tenth, I think, I had one home run, seven RBIs, and was hitting .240." When he set goals, they were clearly articulated and usually numerical. "Look at the statistics," he would say. "Statistics don't lie."

But sometimes they haunt. Brett's 4-for-4, on August 17, sent a tremor through the baseball world. It was thirty-nine years since Ted Williams' .406 season, and baseball minds were generally arrayed against the notion that a contemporary player could match the feat. Night baseball, the invention of the slider, the saturation of the major leagues with strong and crafty relief pitchers—all were given as reasons for the vanishing high-average hitter. Only one player in recent memory had made a plausible run at .400—perennial American League batting champion Rod Carew, who hit .388 for the Minnesota Twins in 1977. But Carew, it was noted, had batted in the .370s through late August: his final .388 reflected a late surge, a peak, and .400 had not really been threatened. And if *Carew* could not hit .400, they said—this wizard of bat control, this magician bunter—then *nobody* could. Certainly not a muscular, nonbunter like Brett with a developing home run stroke and only average speed.

But it was happening. Computer whizzes claimed that the odds against Brett at the beginning of the season had been as low as 2000 to 1 or as high as two billion to one, depending on who you believed; but by August 28, with Brett's average still in the stratosphere and the *possibility* of a .400 season now beyond challenge, the Las Vegas line had dwindled to 4 to 1 against Brett.

"When George first went over .400," recalls the Royals public-relations director Dean Vogelaar, "he and I talked about it after the game. I wanted to prepare him. I knew it was gonna be a crazy time for him the next day in Texas." Vogelaar shakes his head. "But I had no idea. It was unbelievable." When Brett and the Royals checked into the Rodeway Inn in Arlington, Texas, that same Sunday night, the messages and telegrams were already piling up. In addition to the .400 excitement, Brett was also riding a twenty-nine-game hitting streak stretching back to July 18. Premature mention of Joe DiMaggio's record fifty-six-game skein had begun days earlier, and the two themes merged now in a ravenous national appetite for George Brett news. Brett's room phone rang as incessantly as a storefront burglar alarm.

Vogelaar—who, with his imposing size and permed, curly, red-orange hair, bore a happy resemblance to the actor who played the strong man, Sandow the Magnificent, in *The Great Ziegfeld*—flew to Brett's aid the next afternoon, grabbing a travel kit at the office, and catching the first flight to Arlington. "The most difficult thing to handle at first were the TV people," Vogelaar remembers. *Today, Good Morning America,* the network news. They wanted George to take a limo somewhere at four A.M." Vogelaar reluctantly declined for Brett. Eliminated, as well, were telephone interviews, which would have kept Brett shackled to his hotel room wall as securely as irons in a dungeon. Until Vogelaar ordered all of Brett's calls transferred to his room, Brett's dreams were interrupted by reporters, fans, people with business propositions, and sometimes by teenage girls who thought nothing of waking him at 2:00 A.M., just to giggle and hang up. "The best advice I got was from Bob Fishel," Vogelaar says. Fishel, the American League's public-relations director, had been PR man for the New York Yankees in 1961, when a press-tormented Roger Maris had toppled Babe Ruth's single-season home run record. If Brett were to avoid the hounding that Maris had endured, Fishel recommended that press activities be confined, as much as possible, to the ballpark. Vogelaar concurred. And although he and Brett pretty much winged it in Texas, when they got back to Kansas City on Thursday they agreed on a strategy. Brett would submit to a thirty-minute group interview every day—sometime after batting practice—and Vogelaar would allot a few minutes more for scheduled photo sessions and radio-TV interviews. After the game, of course, reporters could interview him at his locker, to ask the ever-popular, "What was the pitch?"

"The difficulty was with *Time, Newsweek, Sports Illustrated, Sport,*" Vogelaar says. National magazines needed exclusive interviews, time to probe Brett's personality; but attempts to satisfy them robbed Brett of quiet lunches on the plane, beers at the Granfalloon (a raucous hamburger and laughs bar in Kansas City's posh Country Club Plaza), or nine holes of golf in the morning. "But George was very patient," Vogelaar said. "He handled it well."

He did more than handle it. He seemed to feed off the media's excitement. Through his thirty-game hitting streak and beyond, in the sweltering heat of July and August of a drought year, when his average climbed to .407, when even his broken-bat bloopers fell in for doubles, Brett had one word for the carnival atmosphere surrounding his exploits. Fun. "This is *fun*," he grinned. "It could end tomorrow, so I'm just trying to enjoy today." The endless questions were like champagne poured over his head in a victory celebration. "It's a problem," he said, "but it's a great problem to have."

Ted Williams, apparently, did not think so. When asked if he thought anybody would hit .400 again, Williams replied testily, "Yes—and I hope somebody does it soon. Then people can start pestering *that* guy with questions about the last guy to hit .400."

Williams saw the irony. His phone rang more often now, with Brett chasing .400, than it had in 1941. In the weeks before Pearl Harbor, Williams' .400 chase had attracted little attention outside of Boston. When New York sports columnist Arthur Daley visited Fenway Park with the Yanks in late September, he expressed surprise at the local enthusiasm. "An amazing degree of interest is being shown in the amazing Mr. Williams," he wrote in a well-hidden column in the back pages of

"I NEVER THOUGHT I'D BE THIS GOOD"

The Times. "A round of applause greets his every appearance at the plate. And when he connects, the ovation is tremendous. One of the local papers carries a daily box on the progress of Williams. Each day a comparison is made of Williams' drive with the memorable .401 accomplishment of Bill Terry in 1930." Of course, a New Yorker could be expected to be patronizing, especially in 1941, which was the year of both Joe DiMaggio's fifty-six-game hitting streak and—that most earth-shattering of events—the Dodgers first pennant since 1920. Interest in Leo Durocher's feisty Dodgers was so great in New York that, despite the fact the Dodgers had clinched the pennant three days earlier, their meaningless last game of the season topped Williams' feat in *The Times:* DODGERS END SEASON WITH 100 VICTORIES: BATTING MARK OF .4057 FOR WILLIAMS. But even in Philadelphia, where the Red Sox closed out the season with a doubleheader against the Athletics, a sparse crowd of 10,268 turned out to witness history in the making. They were rewarded—Williams went 6-for-8, refusing to bench himself to protect his average—but even that drama fizzled when the second game was called on account of darkness with the Athletics leading, 7-1. Hitting .400 was Hall of Fame stuff, to be sure, but the 1941 World Series—won by the Yankees in five games—pushed Williams off the sports pages and into the agate type of the record books. Williams did not even win the Most Valuable Player trophy in 1941. DiMaggio did.

Before 1930, really great hitters *expected* to hit .400 at least once in a career. Shoeless Joe Jackson batted .408 for Cleveland in 1911, but lost the batting title to Ty

Cobb, who hit .420. Rogers Hornsby averaged .402 for the St. Louis Cardinals over a five-year stretch, from 1921-25. Harry Heilmann of the Detroit Tigers set the twenties on fire with seasons of .394, .393, .398, and .403, but is remembered only in trivia tournaments. ("Who the hell is Harry Heilmann?" an amused Brett asked a sportswriter one night.) Sixteen players had hit .400 since major league baseball started play in 1876 (if you excluded the players who did it in 1887, when walks counted as hits). Ty Cobb did it twice and Hornsby did it three times. So did the Yankees Jesse Burkett, who hit .423 in 1895, .410 the next year, and .402 in 1899. (The citizens of Wheeling, West Virginia, Brett's birthplace—if you count Glendale as part of Wheeling—pointed out that he would be their second .400 hitter: Burkett was born there too.) The highest average ever was recorded by Hugh Duffy, the Boston Beaneaters Hall of Famer, who batted .438 in 1894. But his feat is not remembered with the glories of Ruth, Gehrig, Cobb, DiMaggio, Hornsby, and Williams. For one thing, in the 1890s it was not unheard of for an entire league to average .290 or .300 over a season, aided by a rule that fouls didn't count as strikes. In Duffy's glory year, the National League as a whole had a .309 average.

Rules changes deflated batting averages in the first two decades in the 1900s; both the American and National Leagues batted .239 in 1908. But in 1919, a young Boston Red Sox slugger, Babe Ruth, blasted twenty-nine home runs—at the time, a major league record—with what is now known as the "dead ball," a sphere with roughly the resiliency and carrying power of a one-pound bean bag. The following year, wearing a

Yankee uniform and swatting a specially juiced-up ball designed to capitalize on fan fascination with the home run, Ruth hit fifty-four homers, announcing the dawn of the home run era.

Paradoxically, while home run fever is often blamed for the decline in batting averages, the transition period of the 1920s was when the .400 hitter flourished, when Hornsby, Heilmann, and Cobb blistered pitchers in both leagues. The lively ball, launched off the bat of a "hit 'em where they ain't" genius like Cobb, shot past infielders ill-equipped to make diving catches with their tiny, trapless gloves. League batting averages soared, peaking in 1930, when Bill Terry batted .401 and the entire National League hit .303. Little wonder that, to this day, vintage players tend to appraise modern batting averages with contempt. There is a story, perhaps apocryphal, that Ty Cobb was asked at an old-timers' celebration what he would have hit in the modern era. "About .320," Cobb is supposed to have replied.

"That low?" he was asked.

"You've got to remember," Cobb said, "that I'm sixty-four years old."

Cobb's retirement in 1928, followed by Terry's .401 season in 1930, the last in the National League, marked the end of the .400 era. Batting averages declined in 1931, and by 1941, when Williams performed his miracle, the American and National League averages were .266 and .258 respectively. Home run excitement was so alluring that bat control, "hit 'em where they ain't" hitters died out by attrition, replaced by free-swinging, "hit 'em where they sit" sluggers. The trend continued into the seventies, when the so-called "power hitter," capable of sweetening a .220 average with 25 home runs, commanded a hefty salary. In 1966, only two American Leaguers, Frank Robinson and Tony Oliva, topped .300. And in 1968, when the entire league slumped to .230, Carl Yastrzemski won the batting crown with a mere .301—and won it by eleven points, at that. In such a climate, baseball wisdom held, a .400 hitter was as likely as a woman in the White House.

Until Rod Carew.

"Oh, God!" Mike McKenzie groans, his eyes rolling upward. "Rod Carew!"

Mike McKenzie is the unpopular sports columnist of the *Kansas City Times*—known to some as "Mr. Negative"—a bulky, youngish man who looks at life through round, tinted spectacles, and sees it funny. Among his gaffes since joining the *Times* in 1978, critics count the column that accused deer hunters of being animal killers; McKenzie's assertion that drunk Nebraska University football fans who pelted a field with oranges were guilty of bad manners; and his controversial charge that the Kansas City Chiefs, with their single-wing running offense, played dull football. But only a nitwit or a martyr would have opined in Kansas City, in the summer of 1980, that George Brett was not the best hitter in baseball. And that's exactly what Mike McKenzie did.

"All I wrote," McKenzie says with a wan smile, "was that Rod Carew was still the best active hitter in baseball. And, I *believe* it! I think he handles the bat better than Brett does, in terms of bat control and mechanics." Carew, to be sure, boasted a record seven batting titles, eleven consecutive .300 seasons, a .388 season in 1977, and an almost single-handed reintroduction of the lost art of high-average hitting to baseball. (Not to mention the fact that he was still hitting in the .330s for the California Angels, overshadowed by Brett's .400 quest.) "But that opened a wave of criticism from the fans," McKenzie recalls. "I'm not naive. I know readers read into a column what they *want* to read. I understand emotion and all that. But I think it was misunderstood. I definitely didn't say George Brett was no good. People twisted it."

One player who *didn't* seem to resent McKenzie's column was the alleged knockee, George Brett. Not inclined to boast in any event, Brett had a second reason for not taking umbrage; he halfway agreed with McKenzie. From a purely technical standpoint, Carew had been, for years, the standard by which all other hitters were judged. When Brett had won his first batting title in 1976, he had treated it as something of a gift, owed to an "off year" for Carew. Hitters were awed by Carew's bat control, his variety of special stances, his pinpoint bunting, and his machinelike consistency. "He has such great poise," third baseman Brett says. "I play him shallow for the bunt—I'm not gonna *give* him his hits—but time after time he hits ground balls right past me." There were, of course, those who argued that Carew was a Punch-and-Judy hitter, that his generally low run production for the Minnesota Twins was evidence of "empty average." Others insinuated that illness or injury often struck Carew's name from the lineup when a tough right-hander was scheduled to pitch. ("Carew," Blackie Sherrod wrote in the *Philadelphia Inquirer*, "babies his batting average with the tender care of an orchid gardener.") But dissenters were few. Brett rooted for Carew to hit .400 in 1977, and when, for a brief time, it seemed possible that Carew would come to the Royals as a free agent after the 1978 season, Brett predicted that the crafty Panamanian *would* hit .400 on the slick surface of Royals Stadium. "He's got a *wand*," Brett said, "I've got a bat. He's got a magic wand."

Ironically, the last man to hit .400—Ted Williams— had been anything but a tricky batter. A dead pull hitter and a four-time American League home run champion— and therefore a bad example to cite for the deleterious effects of home run hitting on average—Williams had hit thirty-seven home runs to lead the league the year he hit .406. It was *Williams,* some said, against whom Brett should be judged, not Carew. The appeal of *four-zero-zero,* they said, derived from historical mystique: the undemonstrable conviction of the fans of one generation that *their* man—Hornsby, Ruth, Mays, Rose—was greater than the hero of another era. "I think it's harder to hit .400 today than when Williams did it," former Royals (now Yankee) hitting coach Charley Lau might say, but he would be rebutted by an old-timer grousing about how expansion had diluted the major leagues' talent pool. "Artificial turf favors the hitters today," someone else would pipe in. "It makes an infield leakier and discourages outfielders from making diving catches."

"Yeah, and they lowered the mound a few years back," another would say. When baseball men debated the relative degree of difficulty of hitting .400 in 1941 and hitting .400 in 1980, they returned time and time again to these few well-documented changes in pitching styles, strategies, playing surfaces, and travel. But only a very few—Williams among them—seemed to appreciate the one great advantage Williams had enjoyed over Brett: the lack of media pressure.

The electronic media was in its infancy in 1941. There was no television. There were no men with styled hair, outfitted in blazers or plaid sports jackets, standing next to Williams, soberly vacuuming his words with microphones while fiddling with wires dangling from their ears. The giants of the game presumably spoke from time to time, but most fans got news of their heroes secondhand—from the staccato-tongued narrators of the newsreels, or from the gaudy, cliché-ridden prose of newspaper sportswriters. These latter journalists, facing no competition from television and radio, disdained the direct quote. The business of baseball mythmaking was carried on without much involvement by the players themselves, who were free to play cards, drink, talk, squabble, carouse, and talk dirty without interruption. If Arthur Daley could have foreseen the changes television and radio sports coverage would bring, he might have revised his estimate of what constituted "an amazing degree of interest." Rod Carew, in 1977, had buckled under the assault, refusing to travel with the team, wearing disguises, registering under an assumed name at small hotels. Roger Maris, even more shaken by what he considered media harassment during the Ruth-toppling, sixty-one-home-run season, would forever view the press with distaste. "The Yankees didn't do anything but throw me to the wolves," he recalled later. "I couldn't take batting practice, I couldn't do anything. I'd stay for

hours after the game, waiting for everyone to leave."
Brett was now their prey. Shutters clicked wherever he
went. Reporters, when not interviewing him, kept their
eyes on him from a respectful distance, circling anx-
iously like night bugs caught in the stadium lights.
Writers from national magazines followed Brett to the
bat rack, to the trainer's table, and to the shower door,
recording his every profanity and goofy joke for pos-
terity. Others tried to visit his home, to accompany him
on the golf course, to anticipate which beer bar he would
favor on a particular night. "I followed him around for a
few days," confessed Woody Guthrie's biographer, New
York writer Joe Klein, who had been assigned to do a
diary of Brett's .400 quest. "But it was really unplea-
sant. He was getting very uptight with me because
everybody was making demands on him." Klein ultimately gave up on the diary approach, fearful that the
last entry would read, "Brett is looking at me now with
murder in his eyes . . ." "I just wanted to leave him
alone," Klein shrugged.

Media pressure, then—the goldfish bowl phenomenon—was the most agreed-upon argument against
George Brett—or *anyone*—ever hitting .400 again. Nobody argued that it helped. But the other variables of
hitting—all the changes in rules, equipment, and playing conditions that had transformed baseball between
1941 and 1980—remained rich material for debate.
Night baseball, for instance. Baseball wisdom said that
it was harder to see the ball under the lights, and
therefore Williams owned a tremendous advantage over
Brett, who played about 80 percent of his games at
night. Night baseball was also supposedly disruptive of a

player's circadian rhythms, keeping him up to late hours and imposing a lot of red-eye air travel and 3:00 A.M. hotel check-ins. On the other hand, a player like Brett—who for most of his career had partied late and consumed more than his share of postgame brew—surely benefited from the privilege of sleeping late. Players of Williams' era, nursing hangovers, had to squint into an unforgiving noontime sun, their eyes still fuzzy with sleep. Williams also had faced more pitchers, oldtimers noted, in midafternoon, when stadium shadows slashed the area between the mound and home plate—the very worst view of a pitch afforded a batter.

Another bone of contention centered on pitching and defense, which, it was argued, had improved dramatically since Williams' time. A few curmudgeons disputed this, bemoaning again the effects of repeated expansion on the quality of play, but most knowledgeable baseball people agreed that the baseball balance had shifted in favor of the pitchers. The most obvious change was the tactical dominance of the crafty relief specialist, the Rollie Fingers, Goose Gossage, or Sparky Lyle, who entered the game in the late innings to stifle rallies. Starting pitchers in Williams' time often went the distance even when they were hammered for eight or nine runs; but Brett never got to face a floundering pitcher five or six times in one game. What's more, Brett had to face hurlers who teased a hitter with three of four different pitches. Some baseball people attributed the decline in batting averages after World War II to the development of a pitch that Williams never faced: the slider. It was hard to measure the impact of the new breaking pitch on hitters, but few denied that the hard slider had made twenty-game winners out of otherwise so-so fastball pitchers. And deflated batting averages in the process.

Improvements in fielding gloves had also whittled points off the averages of modern hitters. Vintage ball gloves were tiny and webless, resembling the hands of cartoon animals. Old-timers, with justification, heaped scorn upon the massive leather traps worn by modern players. First basemen now smothered low throws in saddlebag-size mitts, robbing fast runners of infield singles. Players made diving catches in the outfield. And pitchers, who used to fend off line drives like a Transylvanian warding off vampires with a crucifix, now wore gloves that snapped shut automatically, denying batters base hits up the middle. If those changes weren't enough to whittle the .400 hitter down to .350, the modern penchant for charting and record keeping had given managers and pitchers a further advantage: documented evidence of a hitter's weaknesses and tendencies. What fields he hit to, broken down by situation, count, and pitch thrown. What pitches he ripped for hits: high fastball, inside curve. What pitches he swung through helplessly—his "hole": anything low and away, any change-up. What pitchers bothered him most: right-handed or left, tall or short, fastball or junk throwers, quick workers or dawdlers. The knowledge that a certain batter invariably hit curve balls hard on the ground to the right of second base encouraged managers to feed the fellow a steady diet of curve balls and position the infielders accordingly. (Pitchers found the "book" of dubious value with a hitter like Williams or Brett, who seemed, like a hungry boarder, to take anything offered.

"The only way to pitch him is inside, so you force him to pull the ball," Yankee pitcher Rudy May said of Brett. "That way, the line drive won't hit you.")

There were, of course, no black or Latin players in the major leagues in 1941, and one writer contended that Williams' average had profited from the racial separatism that befouled baseball in his time. "It's fascinating to wonder what Williams would have done," argued Associated Press sportswriter Doug Tucker, "if he had faced, say Satchel Paige, just ten at bats in 1941, six years before Jackie Robinson broke the color barrier. Paige was pitching for the Kansas City Monarchs in the Negro American League in 1941." Tucker carried it further: "Besides black pitchers, there are black and Latin defensive specialists, like Willie Randolph and Aurelio Rodriguez to make great plays on Brett's line drives. In 1941, they would have been reading about Ted Williams in the newspapers. They would not have been playing against Williams, but they're playing against Brett." Brett allowed that this *was* so, but he would have been unwilling to give up his swings against certain black and Latin pitchers just to avoid Luis Tiant. Ed Figueroa alone was worth about ten points a year to Brett's average. In 1975, when Figueroa was pitching admirably for the Angels, Brett tagged him for thirteen consecutive hits. "We were in Anaheim," Brett recalls fondly, "and I hit a grounder up the middle that Jerry Remy stopped with a dive to throw me out. The Angels dugout gave Figueroa a standing ovation as he came off the field."

There were two variables, unrelated to the changes in baseball, that seemed to favor both Brett and Williams in their .400 drives: injuries and dismal pennant races. On the former, Rod Carew noted that Brett probably profited from the injuries that kept him out of forty-five games in 1980. A player had the best chance of hitting .400, Carew believed, if he came to the plate the minumum number of times required to qualify for the batting crown: 502. The more at bats, obviously, the less likelihood of avoiding that one modest slump that would kill a season's average. In a normal healthy year, such as 1976 when he won the batting title with a .333 average, Brett totaled about 650 at bats—an improbably long span to maintain a steady 2-for-5 pace. Williams, in 1941, missed about two weeks, bolstering Carew's argument. Of course, nagging injuries hamper a player's performance, and the avoid-the-slump argument had to be weighed against the fact that a player injured during a hot streak rarely regained his top form immediately upon coming back—although Brett did so on three occasions in 1980.

The pennant race issue was also a standoff between Brett and Williams. Brett tended to play baseball by the book, at some sacrifice to his statistics: giving himself up to advance runners by hitting to the right of second base with less than two outs. But in 1980, the Royals runaway victory in the American League West left him relatively free to pursue his individual goals. In this light, it is interesting that Williams, Carew, and Brett all produced their highest averages for teams unaffected by pennant races. Williams' Red Sox finished seventeen games behind the Yankees in 1941; Carew's fourth-place Twins trailed the Royals by seventeen and a half in 1977; and the Royals outdistanced second-place Oakland by fourteen games in 1980. Pennant pressure, obviously, did not enhance one's chances of hitting .400.

The debate raged joyously on, particularly in the Midwest, where Brett's quest, chronicled nightly on car and transistor radios, rivaled crickets and locusts for dominance of the night sound. *Fortune* magazine, the business monthly, provided insight into the odds-making process by expounding a formula based on the sparkling career of Rogers Hornsby, who averaged .382 during his peak years, 1920-29. "During those ten years," *Fortune* explained, "he was over .400 three times, but once was as low as .317." Hornsby's "preprogrammed ability," then, was stipulated as .382. "Probability theory tells us that a batting machine programmed to hit .382 has, in fact, a 20.3 percent chance of hitting .400 or more during a season comprising 550 times at bat (about the number of times Hornsby batted in an average season in the 1920s). A 20.3 percent chance in a single season implies a 33% chance of at least three over-.400 seasons in a decade." Moving on to Ted Williams, *Fortune* decided that the Splendid Splinter was at his peak over his first ten seasons, during which he averaged .347. Therefore, by hitting .406 in 456 at bats, Williams beat odds of 118 to 1. Finally, by arbitrarily assigning George Brett a .329 (his 1979 average) for his "preprogrammed ability," *Fortune* gauged that the preseason odds against Brett hitting .400 over 500 at bats had been a forbidding 2300 to 1. Even late in the season, with about 150 at bats left, his chances were only 1 in 12, if he were, in fact, a batting machine (which some pitchers were willing to concede).

Often overlooked in the .400 debate was that Brett

seemed singularly unimpressed by the obstacles arrayed against him. In the torrid weeks of late July and August, when everything Brett hit fell safely, from scorching line drives to seeing-eye rollers, he felt almost infallible. He *knew* he could hit .400. Time, energy, matter, all the playthings of Newtonian physics, seemed favorably arrayed for Brett. He talked confidently of multi-hit games. And why not? Even the laws of *human* nature were reversed. In Texas, Ranger fans cheered his every hit and booed their own pitchers for walking him. In Milwaukee, when Brett's 5-for-5 on August 26 boosted his average to .407, the fans booed the Brewers, but gave Brett standing ovations for his double in the sixth and single in the eighth. Exactly one month later, 11,180 Kingdome fans booed Seattle infielder Larry Milbourne for spearing Brett's shot up the middle and throwing him out at first. Other Mariner players confess disappointment that Brett had not beat up on them as he had on other teams. "I wish he had gone four-for-four," catcher Larry Cox said, "and we still would've won." Only Seattle's rookie manager, Maury Wills, seemed immune to this generous impulse to see Brett hit .400. Wills said, "You don't have time in sports to want the other guy to do well."

The futility of trying to cope with Brett during his hot streak was best expressed by Baltimore manager Earl Weaver one night in Kansas City. Brett had come to the plate in the bottom of the ninth with the score tied, two outs, and Royals on first and second. Rather than risk Brett's bat, Weaver broke the baseball dictum about putting the winning run on third in that situation, and intentionally walked Brett, loading the bases. Weaver then brought in his ace reliever, Tim Stoddard, who *un*-intentionally walked Amos Otis to lose the game. "What's the difference if he beats you with a walk or a hit?" Weaver grumbled afterward. "That's the kind of thing they used to do with Ted Williams, and I'm putting Brett in Williams' class from now on."

In the press box at Royals Stadium, a blue phone would ring twenty or twenty-five times a game. "George Brett's residence," Dean Vogelaar would answer. Without asking who was calling, he would then intone, "two-for-two, a homer and one RBI, .390." Then he would hang up.

Suddenly, in September, the laws of nature reverted to normal. On a road trip to Oakland and Seattle, Brett began swinging at bad pitches. Pitchers began spearing his line drives up the middle, bloopers got caught by diving outfielders, fly balls parachuted to the warning track instead of the bleachers. "He got noticeably tighter," one of the reporters in his entourage recalls. "Short. Snappy. You couldn't stand around the batting cage and shoot the breeze with him anymore."

"I was really very impatient," Brett said later, looking back on his 3-for-20 stretch at the plate. The unprecedented media invasion of his waking hours had not bothered him when he was hot ("It was fun," he admitted. "I don't think I'll ever forget walking into that dome in Seattle for a press conference and finding thirty people waiting."), but the scrutiny was annoying during the slump. "You guys don't seem to understand," he said crankily one night, "that when I go oh-for-four I don't always feel like talking about it." The reporters nodded and wrote that down.

Brett claimed he felt no pressure. "I'm enjoying this," he said, "I really am. I told myself that this might be a once-in-a-lifetime thing and I should enjoy it." But the numbing predictability of the questions was now almost intolerable. *"Do you think you can hit .400? . . . What about .400, George? . . . Will you be disappointed if you don't hit .400?"* Brett's manager, Jim Frey, understood the burden of repetition. "You guys are sympathetic, even apologetic," he told a writer in his office one night, "but you get tired of anything thirty times a day for two months. You get tired of saying the same thing." He smiled weakly. "It's like Lindbergh—he spent ten fucking years talking to people about flying across the ocean."

An incipient immortal like Brett, *Los Angeles Times* columnist Jim Murray wrote, ceased to exist as a person. "You are a phenomenon of nature to be covered like a flood, a channel swim, a man trapped in a cave . . . you get a mental picture of a guy choking to death, 100 feet under ground and the diggers working to get at him and a guy nonchalantly drops a microphone down and says, 'Could you speak a little louder, Floyd, this is network?'"

"It's a terrible dilemma," moaned a Kansas City columnist. "You've done too much with Brett already, but you can't ignore him. Your readers want to read about *Brett.*"

It's symptomatic of the basic writer-athlete relationship," observed Doug Tucker. "We're the people who follow 'em around and write down the funny things they say. They don't really have much respect for us." Al-

37

though usually not noted for their squeamishness, on some nights the reporters clustered around Brett's locker seemed too conscious of each other and of Brett's impatience to function normally. "There's eight guys standing around," UPI Midland's Sports Editor Rick Gosselin recalls with annoyance, "and nobody asks any questions! They just want to be covered in case Brett says anything."

The inevitable result of the extra attention was a sense of isolation from his teammates, physically and spiritually. After a game, Brett had to undress at his locker, tightly ringed by vacant-looking journalists. He might try to look over their heads to make eye contact with a teammate, but the only real remedy was to talk, to acknowledge the listless predators. Often, Brett would volunteer answers to questions that weren't asked, just to make conversation. "Thanks, George," a writer would occasionally say, peeling off from the group. Another would take his place in the ring. "The night in Milwaukee, after the five-for-five," Brett remembers, "the bus had left and I wasn't off my chair yet."

Brett was clearly conscious of the distancing effect, of the resentment this lionization might awaken in his teammates, many of whom were having exceptional seasons, but enjoying less press. "There were nights," Frey recalls, "when Willie Aikens or Willie Wilson had a big game, and George would say out loud, 'Why don't you go talk to somebody else?' George would holler it out loud in the clubhouse. He was getting embarrassed by it." And yet some veteran newsmen considered Brett lucky. Compared to the big-city media, Kansas City journalists were less insistent, more respectful, almost adulatory toward Brett. "Covering the Royals," Gosselin explained, "is like covering the Packers in Green Bay. If he played in Boston, George would have had to go through this the last six years. They have two competing newspapers there, plus the wire services, and they hang on a star's every word. It would have been a nightmare for George." Actually, Brett courted attention, Gosselin said, with his visibility, his gabbiness, his relaxed candor, and his public forays into such realms as presidential politics, highlighted by a September "Town Meeting" appearance in Independence, Missouri. "Did the press ask him to go pose with Jimmy Carter?" Gosselin asked. "That's the biggest spotlight you can put on yourself, standing next to the President of the United States."

Brett tended to agree. "It got to be very, very hectic," he said later. "But it was a great problem to have." He didn't think so, though, in Bloomington, Minnesota. Brooding over his 3-for-20 stretch, Brett, for the first time in his career, refused to talk to the press. "I couldn't believe that when I heard it," Gosselin said in Kansas City. "He's never been like that. George has always been the most cooperative player on the team, the easiest to interview. Win or lose, you knew you could always get a quote from George." The word from Minnesota was that Brett had refused to leave a pepper game for his scheduled half-hour interview session. The Royals traveling secretary, Bill Beck, had reportedly told the waiting, fidgeting journalists, "People, I don't know what to say. He doesn't want to do it today."

"Everybody kinda scatters," recalls Mike McKenzie, who had flown to Bloomington for the weekend. "Very selfishly, I'm still sittin' there in the dugout—'cause he's my Saturday column and I have *nothing*. George plops down next to [Royals catcher] Darrell Porter, and I say, 'You're a helluva guy.' George looks at me casually. I said, 'I spent all of this money, flew all the way to Minneapolis to interview you.'" McKenzie grins. "Which was sort of a white lie, but I'm needling him. 'Not even one question, for God's sake?'

"And Brett looks at me and he looks at Porter and says, 'Darrell, one goddamned day I wanta go without the same questions. One day! What do you think. Do you think there's anything wrong with that?'

"Darrell says, 'There's nothing wrong with that.'

"Brett says, 'See? There's nothing wrong with that. I'll talk to you guys Sunday.'

"I said, 'That doesn't do me any good.' I needled him a little more. 'You don't have a deadline.'

"He says, 'That's kinda tough shit, right?'

"I said, 'For Christ's sake, one question!'

"He says, 'I'm tired of the questions. It's always the same damn questions. "Are you gonna hit .400? Do you think you can hit .400?"'

"And I said, 'Well, I've got an original one that you've never heard before.'

"He says, 'All right, what is it?'

"I said, 'Wait a minute. I gotta think of it.' Well, now he's finally starting to chuckle, loosening up a little. I said, 'Seriously, all I want to know is—are you having fun?'

"And he looks at me and says, 'No.'

"I said, 'Don't you think that's a little odd? Here you are hitting .390, a year most people would give an arm for. You oughta be having the time of your life.'

"He sits there and says, 'Yeah, I know. I talked to [Paul] Splittorff [Royals pitcher] the other day and he's telling me, "George, what if somebody came to you in spring training and said you could hit .380 or .370 and miss forty-five games?" I said, "Yeah, I'da been the happiest guy in the world."' Anyway, my one question . . . he just really poured out some gut-level thoughts. 'This is ridiculous, dammit. *I* didn't set myself up to hit .400. The press did.'

"I said, 'George, you've been set up to fail. If you don't hit .400, you're gonna fail. Isn't that bizarre? You could hit .370 and be a failure!'"

McKenzie smiles. "He came back to me on Sunday and said, 'You know, I've been thinking about what you're saying. I decided to hell with this, I'm gonna have fun.'"

That Sunday, Jim Frey, recognizing that the pressure had finally gotten to Brett, benched him against the Twins. Brett relaxed for the first time in days, tormenting his teammates on the bench with practical jokes. "He's just terrible," Splittorff complained. "Cutting socks, spitting on people's shoes." But when Frey called on Brett as a pinch hitter in the sixth inning, Brett responded with a grand-slam home run. He circled the bases in a cool home run trot, his head modestly bowed, but the kid in him was turning cartwheels again. "I thought it was silly," he said, recalling the euphoria of that slump-breaking homer, "to be one George Brett before the homer and another afterward."

Back in Kansas City, Brett admitted that his dugout conversation with McKenzie had opened his eyes. "I didn't realize what was happening till he told me," Brett said one night before a game with Seattle, contemplating the sorry proposition that his greatest season ever, one of the greatest of all times, might be remembered in negative terms. He leaned back in his director's chair, which had his nickname, "Mullet," printed on the back, and propped his stockinged feet on an empty stool. "Sure, I'm gonna feel bad if I don't make it. If I don't hit .400, the media will make me a goat. They'll probably say that the pressure got to me. People will say that I choked." He shrugged. "I'll be happy if I hit .397, but I'll feel that 1980 was the year that I *almost* hit .400."

"He had built up this goal of hitting .400," Rick Gosselin ventured, "and he started to *fail*. That's why he got depressed and uptight on that road trip. He wasn't failing in the long-term sense, of course. But he had built up his expectations." McKenzie agreed. "He kept convincing himself and convincing himself that he could handle all this . . . and then suddenly he woke up one day and found out, by God, he *couldn't*. It was pissing him off that he was, A, *failing* and, B, having to *explain* it."

"Then it dawned one Sunday," Gosselin said, "when he hit that pinch-hit grand-slam home run, all loosey-goosey . . . he says, 'Geez, why don't I start enjoying baseball.'" Gosselin shrugged. "And then he made a run at it again."

Having cleared the air, Brett went back to the fun business of trying to hit .400. He attacked his goal aggressively, as if listening to an inner voice whispering "no cheap hits." In the last days of the season he went on a power spree, bashing out home runs instead of punching grounders between the infielders. "You'd think a guy trying to hit for average would try to spray it around," manager Frey agreed, not at all displeased with Brett's blasts into the Royals bullpen. "But you always have to go back to how they're pitching him."

That's *when* they pitched him, of course. On the last road trip, Brett faced a few minor league pitchers up for a September look: wild, lanky youngsters unfamiliar to him. He also ran a gauntlet of left-handers. (Fans tend to disbelieve in the "hallowed percentages," but Brett hit .437 against right-handers in 1980, and a more human .318 against left-handers—a difference of 119 points.) "He just wasn't getting the pitches," Wathan says of the last days of the season, when Brett's goal slipped just beyond his reach. "Instead of getting four swings, four at bats a game, he was really getting two. He'd walk once or twice." Sometimes it was strategy: opposing managers didn't want Brett to beat them. Other times it was too-careful pitching by cautious hurlers.

"I was pulling like hell for him, except when he was playing the Yankees," Charley Lau said. Earlier in the year, Lau had been quoted to the effect that his protégé would never hit .400, great as he was. Lau said he had been misquoted. "I said, 'If anybody *could* do it, *he* would. There's nothing that George does with a bat that surprises me. If George's goal was .400 and winning had nothing to do with it—" Lau hesitated. "I think he could."

Although *four-zero-zero* slipped away, another statistic loomed large. For weeks, Brett had averaged over one RBI per game. The last player to maintain that average while batting in over 100 runs in a season was Walt Dropo, who had totaled 144 in 136 games for Boston in 1950. Brett accomplished that feat in 1980, driving in

118 runs in 117 games. Thus, as the .400 frenzy receded in the last three or four games, as the *Newsweek* crew packed up and flew back to New York, as the network bigwigs prepared for the play-offs and the World Series—the long view became possible again. The weight of Brett's season became suddenly more profound, measured against the brilliant seasons of the men he had eclipsed in 1980: the Yankees Reggie Jackson, who had produced his greatest season ever, batting .300 with 41 homers, and 111 RBIs; Milwaukee first baseman Cecil Cooper, who had turned in a devastating .352 campaign, with 219 hits, 25 homers, and 122 RBIs; and the Royals own brilliant young outfielder, Willie Wilson, who had stockpiled 230 hits, 133 runs, a .326 average, and 79 stolen bases. (Discerning fans pointed out a symbiotic relationship between Brett and the awesomely fast Wilson: Willie got on and George drove him in. Was it mere coincidence that Brett had blossomed as an RBI man in 1979, the year Wilson had become a starter?) "Before I came back to the National League I said Brett was the best player in the American League," said St. Louis Cardinals manager Whitey Herzog, Brett's former manager with the Royals. "Now that I've seen both leagues, I say he's the best there is." Royals designated hitter, Hal McRae, who had played with future Hall of Famer Pete Rose in Cincinnati, was asked to compare Brett with Rose. "The only difference," McRae laughed, "is that George is larger than Pete, he's stronger than Pete, and he's faster than Pete." The Royals young shortstop, U. L. Washington, also seemed capable of the long view. "It's somethin', just sittin' over there watching him hit the ball like that," Washington said. "I guess

guys who played with Ted Williams felt the same thing. It'll be great to look back on, to be able to say, 'Hey, I played next to George. He hit .390 and I saw every bit of it.'"

The long view.

"There is no such thing as a .400 hitter," Thomas Boswell wrote in the *Washington Post*. "There is only a great hitter who has swum out farther than he ever has before and then must tread water as long as his strength and luck can last."

2. Aura

Autumn drama.

All eyes were on George Brett. He assumed a very wide stance, rocking his weight from side to side, like an elephant's trunk. His chewing tobacco tin was outlined in his back pocket. He stood poised in bright sunshine; the other players watched from the shadows.

"Bet he fouls it off," muttered a pale young man in the crowd. His girlfriend, wearing a GEORGE BRETT FOR PRESIDENT T-shirt, nudged him in the ribs.

Suddenly, Brett swung—violently—and a second after impact he *yelped*. You could hear it a hundred yards away. The ball was still rising and Brett stood stockstill, his hands raised in triumph, watching it fly. "That's gonna make it!" he yelled in amazement. Then he screamed: *"Fore!"* Players on the distant green crouched and covered their heads.

A moment later he was clowning. He hooted, "Robin *who?*" and flopped down in a golf cart next to his curvacious brunette chauffeur.

One of Brett's playing partners laughed. "Robin Yount," he said, naming the Milwaukee Brewers shortstop who was one of the guests at the Peter Marshall Celebrity Golf Tournament in Kansas City. "Yesterday we were teamed with Yount, who's a very good golfer, and today George won't let us forget it. Every time he hits a good shot, he says, 'You're gonna forget you ever *heard* of Robin.'"

On the third tee, Brett glanced at a sponsor's sign which proclaimed a LONGEST DRIVE contest. "What do you get if you get the longest drive?" he asked, brandishing his driver menacingly.

The girl in the T-shirt chewed her nails. "A night with George Brett," she murmured.

When the hole was clear, Brett teed up and glared down the tree-lined fairway. "I feel very confident of this next shot," he announced. *"Very* confident." He planted his feet again in that wide stance—much wider than his baseball stance—and shifted his weight back and forth. "More cash for my pocket," he said. "I need new shoes." He suddenly coiled and attacked the ball with a vicious swing, grunting loudly at impact. The ball rocketed on a perfectly straight line, dead center of the fairway, too far out for most of the applauding gallery to follow. In the distance, a man in a blue Windbreaker ran out, uprooted a little orange flag, advanced a few yards toward the green, and planted it next to Brett's ball.

Brett's grin was almost as broad as it had been the night he launched Goose Gossage's most regrettable fastball into the third tier of Yankee Stadium for the three-run homer that had sealed the 1980 American League pennant for the Royals—their first. He sat in his golf cart with his feet up, signing autographs, as relaxed as a young rajah being fanned by native girls. Comedian Tom Poston, wearing a Mork and Mindy sweater, approached the third tee, one suspicious eyebrow raised. "Don't you guys have a celebrity?" he commiserated.

In truth, all Kansas City suddenly had a celebrity, its biggest ever (if you conceded Harry Truman to nearby Independence). These were joyous times for Brett. Instead of hiding out at his very private Lake Quivira, Kansas, retreat—scorching steaks and chickens for a few close friends—Brett popped up everywhere, sometimes in unlikely costumes: downtown, riding a horse, in the Kansas City pennant celebration; clowning with a trombone at a Liberty Memorial victory rally; toting a shotgun through russet foliage behind bounding hunting dogs and ahead of TV cameras; enduring a celebrity roast; winning a fifth-place ribbon for his Arabian horse at the American Royal; throwing the switch for 100,000 Kansas Citians witnessing the annual illumination of the Christmas lights on the Country Club Plaza; posing in a hockey uniform to publicize a movie role. His greatest season had earned him his second American League batting championship, the Most Valuable Player Award, about two trophy cases worth of lesser tributes, and sudden elevation to the highest ranks of baseball stardom. Brett was savoring his winter of triumph. "He knows he's great now," teammate Clint Hurdle said. "He *knows* he's the best baseball player in the American League. How much better can he be, after last season?"

*   *   *

Eight months before, a writer had set out to ask Brett that very question. He drove through the snow-covered wooded hills of extreme eastern Kansas on a snow-blinding, blue-sky day in March, 1980. It was the worst possible time to do an article on a baseball player, he thought, as he squinted over the glare-flashed hood at ambiguous landmarks and unreadable road markers. Players were packing for spring training, getting in a last weekend of hunting, or winding up their tours of duty on the rubber-chicken circuit. Back at Royals Stadium, snow blanketed the evergreen carpet: the crowned monolith scoreboard was dark and lifeless, save for the clock that burned infinite, like a doorbell light. The clubhouse was empty, the press box a sterile curve of unblemished countertops. In the executive offices, secretaries checked their watches every five minutes and groaned.

It was hard to reach people. Hal McRae was in Bradenton, Florida. Billy Martin was unavailable. Charley Lau had not yet returned his call—if he had gotten any message at all. Whitey Herzog, unemployed, was cheerfully prowling the Missouri landscape with his hunting dogs. Al Zych, the clubhouse manager—and one of Brett's favorite people—was already in Fort Myers, Florida, preparing the spring training headquarters. In fact, the only contact the writer had made, so far, was then Chicago White Sox owner Bill Veeck, who was reportedly a great admirer of Brett's. "Yes, hello?" Veeck had answered, sounding like a passerby hesitantly picking up the receiver in a phone booth. "What can I do for you?" When the writer had explained his assignment,

"I NEVER THOUGHT I'D BE THIS GOOD"

Veeck's voice had crackled over the phone: "I think he's just about as good a hitter as there'll ever be." (The writer liked that! Not "as good a hitter as there *is*," or "ever *was*," but "as good as there ever will *be*.") In Veeck's mind the most vivid memory of George Brett was of the afternoon in Yankee Stadium, in the 1978 American League championship series, when Brett had blasted three home runs in one game off Jim "Catfish" Hunter. "His style was influenced by his hitting coach," Veeck had said, referring to Charley Lau, "and by the terrain on which he played," referring to the slick, hard playing surface of Royals Stadium, "but I think he gave an example that day in New York of what he could do if he tried for the long ball." Veeck had hesitated. "Do you need more? How's this?" There was a long pause. "I've always lived in mortal fear"—he had seemed to savor the words *mortal fear*—"that he would go for the downs against us." Veeck had sounded very satisfied with himself. "Is that good?"

"That's wonderful," the writer had replied.

But he needed more than pithy testimonials for a good article. He needed scenes. Players cracking jokes around the batting cage, managers putting their stockinged feet up on the managerial desk, relief pitchers letting the air out of the tires on the bullpen car, bleacher fans throwing beach balls and flashlight batteries at the unpopular right fielder. Those scenes weren't to be had in mid-March, when the average ballplayer was wallpapering his kitchen nook or driving his dog to the vet's. The writer wished he had written down all the George Brett scenes he had witnessed over the years, recorded the funny dialogue, kept a log. But he hadn't. He had interviewed Brett five or six times for articles about *other* Royals—he was the best interview on the team, by far, full of spontaneous fun and gab, a stream-of-consciousness outpouring of baseball analysis and light-hearted character assassination—but on those occasions, Brett had talked little about himself. The writer particularly regretted not having stalked him to one of his late-night lairs in Kansas City's Westport district, where his reputation as a ladies man and prolific drinker—if you could believe the second- and thirdhand testimony of the Westport crowd—had spawned. (A St. Louis writer had gathered some juicy stuff about Brett by hanging out, after night games, in the alley alongside a singles bar called The Happy Buzzard, where sinewy young women and star-stuck kids maintained a feverish vigil for Kansas City's most eligible bachelor.) The rustic landscape the writer was driving through now did not promise any such lode of atmosphere: the most he hoped for was that Brett might be building a snowman in the yard.

The entrance to Lake Quivira Estates was a more elegant version of an army-camp gate. A uniformed guard, after checking his clipboard for approved visitors, gave the writer a pass to display in his window and gave him a few simple directions to Brett's house—involving a drive past the boathouse, a brief skirting of the frozen lake, a right fork up a steep hill through houses and trees—and dispatched him with a "You can't miss it." Minutes later, the writer was lost, backing out of wooded cul-de-sacs and turning around in people's driveways. He encountered no traffic and spied no humans during his search: just garage doors, tarpaulined canoes and snow-capped barbecue ovens.

Luckily, the mailbox at the end of one empty driveway

"I NEVER THOUGHT I'D BE THIS GOOD"

said G. BRETT. The writer parked on the shoulder and stepped out into the frosty air. The house was a small fieldstone chalet, almost obscured by trees, nestled in the hillside overlooking the lake. The writer crossed a redwood footbridge, looking everywhere for signs of life, and approached the front door tentatively, afraid that his finger on the doorbell would jar the woodsy tranquillity and bring angry faces to the window. But he needn't have worried. The doorbell brought nothing.

He stared at his size 13 feet for a while, listening for telltale thumps from inside, and then pressed the button again, more insistently, letting the ring echo inside.

Nothing.

He had talked to Brett on the phone at about eleven o'clock that morning. "Yumph?" Brett had answered sleepily. The writer had apologized for waking him, although it was, in fact, the exact hour Brett had asked him to call. "No, that's okay," Brett had mumbled "that's how I get up. . . . Why don't you come out around one?"

The writer looked at his watch: it was 1:05.

He walked back to his car and stared down the road, thinking that Brett might suddenly sweep into view in one of the Porsches he hawked on Kansas City television. Shivering, the writer got in the car and turned on the radio. It was a long drive back into town, and he hated to give up on the interview. Brett was flying East the next morning to tape some commercials for a chewing tobacco, and from there he was traveling straight to the Royals camp in Fort Myers. It was now or never.

After about ten minutes, the writer got back out of the car and crossed the footbridge again. This time, after ringing the bell, he pounded on the door with his gloved hand, producing a rather dull thump. He stared at his feet again, composing a silent curse on all ballplayers, their heirs and assigns, and was just turning to leave when the door suddenly cracked open. There stood a stunningly beautiful young woman in an elegant, layered negligee.

"Come on in," she said with a warmth usually reserved for meter readers and process servers. She rustled, padding barefoot across the carpet, as she led the writer to a sunken living room. "You can wait here," she said. "He's still in the shower." Then she walked back to the bedroom, never to reappear.

The writer was unprepared for Brett's living room. He had braced himself for beer can pyramids, a hide-a-bed and K Mart end tables—an absurd vision, for Brett earned several hundred thousand dollars a year, and had recently moved out of a Ward Parkway mansion; but his bachelor reputation, his adolescent pregame antics and—dare we say it—his *locker,* which was a vertical landfill of dirty laundry, odd toys and gifts, baseball cards, and pinups, prophesied the digs of a surfer type living near the cove at La Jolla, California. (Cindy Boren, writing in the *Kansas City Star* a year or two earlier, had championed the messy-bachelor theme by reporting that Brett's mother, visiting from California, had felt compelled to attack a mountain of orphaned laundry. "Fifteen loads," his mother was quoted as saying. "I think I did fifteen loads.") But no. Brett's Quivira Lake living room looked like a photograph in a designers' magazine—an uncluttered, tasteful, Danish modern interior, all browns and beiges. An imposing stone fireplace dominated one wall; expensive framed lithographs, horse racing and baseball scenes, provided some color; paperweights and table sculptures lent their studied presence to horizontal surfaces; sliding glass doors to a sun deck provided a glorious view of the frozen lake and the wooded ridge beyond. There were only two noticeable lapses: a Royals batting helmet perched on the stereo receiver, and a two-year-old copy of *Sports Illustrated* on the coffee table—the issue with Royals outfielder Clint Hurdle on the cover.

Brett appeared five minutes later, clad in a blue jogging suit and athletic shoes. He had apparently combed his brown-blond hair with a towel; he scratched his stomach sleepily, like Wallace Beery in a half-dozen movies. He had shaved, fighting his never-ending battle against a beard that cast a five-o'clock shadow at three o'clock. "Hi," he yawned, settling onto the sofa, his arms draped over the back and his legs stretched past the coffee table. "What's this for?"

The writer had explained over the phone—twice, actually—that he was doing a cover story on Brett for *Sport* magazine—but Brett had apparently forgotten. He gave no indication, either, that he recognized the writer from previous interviews. That no longer surprised the writer. Brett was familiar with the regular beat reporters who covered the Royals and with the television reporters who had stood beside him a hundred times for minicam reports at the ballpark. But he took no more notice of out-of-town reporters and magazine writers than he did of the pencil-clutching hoards of autograph seekers that he bantered with in the stadium parking lot every night. "How does it work?" he asked, after the writer had again explained his purpose. "Do they just call you and say, 'Go write about this guy'?"

"Yeah," the writer said, "sort of." For some reason, he didn't know what to make of the question. Brett had never betrayed an interest in the editorial mechanics of the magazine business. ("I've read two books in my life," he once told a reporter, *"Basketball Sparkplug and Love Story.")* So he was doubtless making small talk. But something still struck the writer as strange about the question. As the interview proceeded, it finally hit him: *It was a rookie's question.* Brett, as a five-time All-Star and a former American League batting champion, had been featured before by all the major sports magazines—usually after sessions with free-lancers like himself—and the writer had naturally assumed that these sessions were old hat to him, tiresome even. And yes, he *looked* bored with his legs stretched out and his limp arms draped like a scarecrow's. But the way Brett rambled, the quick jumps of subject matter, the easy profanity, the self-deprecation—everything gave the impression that the talk was a pleasurable novelty. The writer was reminded that professional athletes in Kansas City, to a man, complained that the Midwest was a publicity vacuum, neglected by the national media and the big-bucks advertisers. Great players like Cecil Cooper, Amos Otis, and St. Louis shortstop Garry Templeton, the argument went, played second fiddle to the heavily hyped stars of New York, Los Angeles, Philadelphia, and Boston—the Reggie Jacksons, Steve Garveys, Pete Roses, and, Lord help us, even the Bucky Dents. Recalling a *Sport* editor's assertion that Brett was probably the most underrated player in baseball, the writer decided to probe Brett's feelings on the subject.

"Do you think you're underrated?" he asked.

Brett looked surprised. "No, I don't feel like I'm underrated at *all. . . ."* He shook his head. "My last contract, that I signed in seventy-six—I was among the top ten paid. That's not being underrated. I was only twenty-three years old at the time." He searched for a more salient measure of his worth. "When I go to New York, they *hate* me . . . which means they think I'm a good player. You know, they hate good players." He looked thoughtful. "And a lot of places I go, people are always screamin' at me, and that means they like me . . . or *dislike* me, I really don't know. But it seems like everywhere I go, people know who I am. I get a lot of recognition for someone playing in Kansas City."

Brett's speech was a hurried, slightly blurred California tongue, which for too long had had to compensate for cheeks stuffed with pink bubble gum and chewing tobacco. Now he spoke in a murmur, as if reluctant to disturb the profound hush of the sun-drenched room. The stillness was almost eerie. "In the daytime, this is the most peaceful place I've ever lived," he said. "It's fantastic. People ask me where I live and I say Kansas. They say, *'Kansas!?* What the hell do you live in Kansas for?' But I love it, it's really me. I've kinda acclimated myself to the Midwestern way of life. Some days I like to go lay on the dock. Take my little cassette player down there and play music. Some days I like to go out and play nine holes of golf. Today I don't know *what* the hell I'm gonna do." He stared out at the frozen lake. "Not much you can do today!" He looked around the room. "I've lived in this house since last May third, and I imagine there haven't been more than twenty people in it. Twenty different people." He cocked his head. "I've become kind of private."

Private?

Had public speculation about his sex life, his drinking habits, and—yes—even his laundry and housekeeping routines driven Brett underground? Was he, as cynics would suggest, burned out? Was it agoraphobia? Or was it, as the writer suspected, that Brett was now becoming aware of his own potential as a player, and was somewhat awed?

"I never thought I'd be this good," Brett admitted. "I never thought I'd hit .300. I never thought when I first signed my contract out of high school in seventy-one that I'd make it to the major leagues. I mean, every kid wants to be a major league baseball player, but in reality, can they be?" His eyebrows lifted. "Can they be? I was gonna play five years in the minors and if I didn't make it to the major leagues I was gonna quit. And what I'd probably be doing now, is working for my brother John, hammering nails . . . or, a friend of mine has a restaurant out in LA . . . being bartender for him. Whatever." He shook his head. "So far, my career has been a total surprise."

The writer and Brett talked about a lot of things that afternoon—the science of hitting, the art of relaxation, the childish nature of professional ballplayers—but two things stuck in the writer's mind: Brett's phrase, "I never thought I'd be this good," and the heavy quiet of Brett's ice palace. As Brett answered his questions, the writer stared out the glass doors at the wooded ridge and the frozen lake below, dusted with virgin snow. He suddenly felt as if he had wandered into a scene from an Ingmar Bergman movie—a static tableau, a droning voice-over, a motionless figure almost offscreen.

"It's very peaceful," Brett said. "The wintertime is great." He appraised, without interest, the expensive prints and lithographs on his walls. He said, "I'm very happy."

Hindsight. It is easy, looking back on that quiet winter afternoon, to see that George Brett was poised on the brink of national celebrity. Brett himself was only dimly aware of the energy building up behind his name throughout the year: the simultaneous courtship of reporters from various national magazines, the sudden interest from national advertisers, the endorsements, the television commercials. "It just suddenly exploded," he said in late May, commenting on the multiple burst of George Brett magazine covers that had just hit the newsstands. He seemed a little baffled by the sudden attention, but not at all bothered. "I don't know how to account for it," he shrugged, attributing the sudden flow of ink to the bandwagon psychology of media people. Kansas City fans were less charitable. "It's about *time*," they huffed. "What does a guy have to do to get a little recognition?"

A few words about Kansas City. It is a militantly provincial city in which half the population affects the fashion and sophistication of upper-crust New York and the other half deflects unwelcome comparisons with the disclaimer, "We may not be as fashionable and sophisticated as those stuck-up New Yorkers, *but . . .*" Kansas Citians feel unappreciated. Or worse: misrepresented. Their city is one of the more beautiful in America: hilly, heavily wooded, with extensive tendrils of landscaped boulevard that wind gracefully through neighborhoods of unusual charm; yet they anguish over their cow-town image, over the Eastern conceit that everything west of Cleveland is a treeless plateau populated solely by tumbleweeds, ranch hands and slat-ribbed steers. Provincialism is a rap, of course, and most Kansas Citians squawk at the accusation, even when they've been caught making too much of the fact that Ernest Hemingway was a *Kansas City Star* reporter for a few months in his youth, that Walt Disney lived there, that Jean Harlow was born there, or that Kansas City is the greeting card capital of the world. The *Kansas City Star/ Times* routinely rewrites Associated Press dispatches to identify golf great Tom Watson as "Kansas City's Tom Watson." Relief pitcher Neil Allen, when he survives a ninth-inning crisis in Shea Stadium, is soberly identified as "a former Wyandotte High School star."

The national media, of course, do not share this perspective of a world bounded on the west by Wichita, on the east by Columbia (halfway to St. Louis), on the north by Omaha (home of the Royals Class AAA farm club), and on the south by 165th Street (Snead's Barbecue). Their perspective, Kansas Citians charge, approximates Steinberg's famous aerial view of Manhattan's West Side, with Jersey City just across the Hudson River . . . and Pittsburgh, Nebraska, Kansas City, San Francisco, Russia, and Japan penned in uncertainly in the wasteland beyond. It infuriates Kansas Citians when Howard Cosell eulogizes Yankee second baseman Willie Randolph at the obvious expense of the Royals Frank White, or when Yankee pinstripes dominate the covers of national sports magazines. After a deluge of complaints about announcer bias during the 1980 play-offs, an exasperated ABC sports executive said of Kansas City fans, "They haven't got a chip on their shoulders—it's a giant redwood."

With this as background, it is easy to understand how suspicious Brett's fans were of his sudden lionization. It had been a truism that Kansas City players didn't get national endorsements, but suddenly there was George Brett getting his uniform dirty for Lifebuoy Soap ("After I give my body to baseball . . . I give my body to Lifebuoy") or modeling his bulging cheeks for Union Station Chewing Tobacco. The St. Louis Cardinals first baseman Keith Hernandez and the California Angels designated hitter Don Baylor—voted their league's MVPs for 1979—weren't getting the attention Brett was. Even Pittsburgh patriarch and slugger Willie Stargell, who had led his "Family" of Pirates to World Series victory in 1979, could not crowd Brett out of the picture. *Baseball Digest* named Brett its 1979 Player of the Year, citing his twenty-plus doubles, triples, and homers in a single season, which had been accomplished only four times, the last time by Willie Mays in 1957. *Baseball Bulletin* had agreed, making Brett their "runaway choice" for Player of the Year for "one of the finest all around seasons in baseball history"—a .329 average, 119 runs, 107 RBIs, and a league-leading 212 hits.

A bemused Brett likened his jump in status to an "explosion," but to his new manager, Jim Frey, the interest was more of a blossoming. "You can't go out and *demand* respect and recognition," Frey said late in the season. "You have to start putting statistics and records together. The record spotlights a performance and the media picks up on it." Frey's voice was emphatic: "But the performance has to come first. There's been a million guys who've had the *potential*—but never put the statistics together. George has done it long enough for people to say he is one of the best, if not *the* best player in the American League. And it came to bloom in 1980."

Frey's remarks subtly rebuked those fans and players who—after complaining for years about Brett's lack of national publicity—now contended he was getting too much. The theme was timeless. The star system had always stirred oceans of resentment in certain fans, who often came in one of two shapes: the *kindergarten teachers,* who knew that little Billy's feelings would be hurt if little Georgie got all the love and attention ("Pete LaCock [Royals former first baseman] may not hit as many home runs as George Brett does, but he *tries* just as hard, and it isn't fair that he doesn't get to play"); and the *egg throwers,* who were usually devoted to some rival team or player ("George Brett couldn't fill Pete Rose's shoes with a shovel"). The temptation—Frey succumbed—was to explain, quietly and rationally, that great young players like Willie Wilson couldn't expect enshrinement in the Hall of Fame on the strength of two fine seasons, and that Brett's career accomplishments *did,* in fact, set him apart from his teammates. But the effort was pointless. The outbreak of leveling sentiment merely confirmed that Brett had reached the top of his profession. "I've never seen anybody play as well as he's played," Frey said, searching his memory for a performance to rival Brett's 1980 season. He shrugged helplessly.

"I NEVER THOUGHT I'D BE THIS GOOD"

"There's a lot of resentments that teammates can't be open with," one reporter pointed out, "because they know George's fame is deserved. Luckily, George handles it beautifully. If George were a jerk, like Reggie, in the same circumstances . . ." The thought went uncompleted.

John Wathan, too, saw the pitfalls. "There were times, I'm sure, some guys got a little upset," he said the following winter. "Other guys were having outstanding seasons—we hit the highest average in the American League in thirty years—but there were no writers around." In the clubhouse, certain Royals sometimes chided reporters with digs like, "Did you come to write about the Kansas City Bretts?" But generally they admired Brett as a "teamer" and a regular guy—and as leverage toward a World Series check. (As Royals broadcaster Fred White put it, "Do you want George Brett on your club hitting .400? . . . or on somebody *else's* club hitting .400?")

Mindful of the resentment potential, the Royals organization would not sell George Brett souvenirs at the ballpark, or market their product with his image, as did KMBZ radio, which billed itself as "The home of George Brett excitement." "We don't want to promote one player over the others," marketing director Bryan Burns explained. "Unless an item is licensed by the Major League Baseball Players Association, we do not stock that item for sale in the ballpark. Some clubs have Joe Blow Poster Day. I don't think we'd do that." The exception was a George Brett T-shirt, sold with all the players' consent at the height of .400 interest, and with all the players receiving a royalty. Promoters were calling daily with marketing ideas (Burns's favorite was the George Brett lunch box), and although Brett controlled the rights to his name and likeness, the Royals, in most cases, could command a percentage of the wholesale price. "If he appears in his uniform—even his cap—we have a secondary interest," Burns said. The Royals, for instance, earned a royalty on Brett's commercials for 7-Up and Lifebuoy.

Brett's marketability in Kansas City, long the envy of his teammates, was magnified by his growing national stature. Brett's July appearance at Jerry Hays Ford in Independence—one of those feeble promotions where a ballplayer hands out autographed pictures in a showroom while car salesmen work the crowd—attracted three thousand people, with people and cars spilling out on the street in a massive traffic jam. In a more inspired scheme, Home Savings and Loan Association planned for Brett, recently named a vice-president, to attend every home settlement and sign the contract for the bank, "so that buyers will get Brett's autograph merely by purchasing a $60,000 house." According to the association's president, Ray Gifford, "It might be just what the home market needs."

No wonder there was often a note of resentment in certain Royals assertions that Kansas City was "Brett's town." "If we were in business, going *out* to get things," Burns said, "they'd be justified." But the Royals, he said, did not solicit promotional opportunities for players. "We just handle it when the phone rings. We won't even recommend a player. We say, 'You tell us who you want.'" Usually, they wanted Brett, which Burns attributed to Brett's personality and to his brilliant performances in nationally televised postseason games. "When Howard Cosell sticks a mike in your face, some guys go stiff as a board. George isn't that way. He comes across. He doesn't hide anything. He wears his feelings on his face very well."

If the Royals secretly envied Brett's expanding wealth and reputation, they certainly did not envy the uncomfortable scrutiny he suffered with it. It was the best kind of World Series drama when Brett got up from his hospital bed after a hemorrhoid operation and blasted a first-inning homer in the third game of the 1980 series. But his intimate misery mostly brought down upon him a rain of wisecracks from talk show hosts and anally enlightened columnists. At St. Luke's Hospital in Kansas City, letters and telegrams had poured in from as far away as Hawaii—enough material for a book of folk remedies. Enough for a gag book, as well. One woman had sent Brett a get-well tree decorated with empty Preparation H boxes. "My problems are behind me now," Brett joked in the clubhouse, but his edginess showed. "It's a very embarrassing problem," he told a four-deep throng of sportswriters. "I tried to keep it a secret and I was very disappointed when it came out in the paper."

In Babe Ruth's time, old-timers noted, the Yankees would have told the press that the Bambino had a tummyache from too many hot dogs and bottles of soda pop. Not so with Brett. During batting practice, before the fifth game of the World Series, a television cameraman followed behind him so closely that Brett was afraid to turn quickly for fear of being struck. Brett finally ducked into the sanctuary of the batting cage. "What are you trying to get?" he said, trying to hide his annoyance. "A shot of my ass?"

The respectful distance of the black-and-white, pre-sound era had shrunk to a pickpocket's reach.

"What people see now is the finished product," Hal McRae said one afternoon, watching a hatless, sweating George Brett take his swings in the batting cage. "They didn't see him when he was rough."

"You don't think he was a natural?" someone asked.

McRae sidestepped the question. "He was a big guy. He could run. He had a good arm and he was an adequate fielder. He had a chance to be a good hitter—" McRae shrugged. "But you didn't know."

Brett lashed a hard grounder toward the mound; the ball rebounded off the protective screen and vaulted high and back over the batting cage. "Heads up!" Brett yelled. He grinned as reliever Dan Quisenberry fell to his knees, shielding his head with his arms.

McRae said, "He used to have trouble fielding, but he doesn't have trouble now. He worked very hard."

"I was never a good fielder in the minor leagues," Brett explained. He looked at his hands, streaked with pine tar and yellowed with callouses. "I was a catcher in high school for a while. I liked catching; you were always in the ball game. At third base you just stand there and they hit the ball at you. My favorite third baseman, when I hit the majors, was Brooks Robinson. I was number five for that reason. I remember the first time Brooks hit me a ball, I didn't know what to do. I threw the ball twenty feet wide." He leaned over and spit on the dugout steps. "I think my favorite third baseman now is Richie Hebner." Noting the surprised reaction of his listener, Brett shrugged. "He's not noted for his fielding—he's real erratic, like I am. He's just a fantastic guy. He's in a world by himself. A lot of people think he's nuts, he's crazy, whatever, but whether he goes four-for-four or oh-for-four, he's got peace of mind. Yeah, he's one of my all-time favorites. Mickey Stanley is another of my favorites."

Brett had never bragged about his fielding, but from the beginning fans had recognized him as one of the most exciting third basemen in baseball—particularly if they sat in the box seats behind first base, where many of Brett's scorching throws ended up. Those boxes became known as a "hard-hat area," and Brett labored long to shed his scatter-arm tendencies. "I just didn't have much confidence in my fielding," Brett said. "I made a few errors, and got a little defensive out there. I was saying, 'Hit the ball to Freddie, hit the ball to Frank.'" The hot corner demanded a bomb squad temperament, but Brett's was a playful nature, longing to relax. "Sometimes I'm scared," he admitted. "The ball's gonna come and I'm not gonna catch it." The outfield, one gathered, might better suit Brett's personality. "I'd play first! I'm not an egotist. It breaks up the monotony of going out to the same place every day. I'll play right field." He laughed harshly. "I said once, 'If I stay healthy, I have a chance to become the first player ever to collect three thousand hits and one thousand errors.'"

There was only one thing wrong with Brett's devastating critique of his own fielding: it was several years out of date. Although not a Gold Glover, he was capable of inspired play at third—blocking balls with his chest, rifling throws across the infield, one-handing bunts, hurling himself on the dugout roof after pop fouls. "I'm a lot more confident now," he conceded, unwilling to risk thunderbolts by actually boasting.

"He had to prove to himself that he could play in the field," McRae said, "which maybe he didn't believe. He always had a lot of ability in the field, but he would make mistakes. He might throw it away. But just this year, after the All-Star break, it seemed like everything fell in place." McRae added, "He always worked hard on his fielding."

Work.

"I first saw George in the instructional league in 1971," said former Royals pitching star Steve Busby. "He was working with Steve Boros then on his third-base play, but at that point, to tell you the truth, nothing really impressed me about him. He was just a maturing kid, not a whole lot above average." John Wathan, who met George Brett the following spring, had been only a little more impressed than Busby. "I recognized that he had a lot of talent," Wathan says, "but I never dreamed that he'd be the ballplayer that he is today."

So . . . what happened?

"He just kept getting better," says one of Brett's high-school teammates. "George is one of the few guys I've known that has gotten better at every level of competition."

Yes, but why? Everyone shrugs.

John Schuerholz is the director of player personnel for the Kansas City Royals. He is a trim, fast-talking executive with the hair and profile of a screen actor and a brain packed with impressions and raw data on every player who has ever passed through the Royals organization. He alone seems to remember George Brett as something more than just a fair prospect. "Nobody could honestly project George Brett to be a .390 hitter,"

Schuerholz said one spring morning in his office at Terry Park in Fort Myers. "He was a heavy-legged, not ideally built player. And he had a stance that was a replica of Carl Yastrzemski's. But he always showed good mechanics. The thing that struck me about George"—Schuerholz looked at the ceiling, reflecting——"was an intangible quality. He looked like he was as determined and hardworking as anybody who ever came into the game. That inner quality, that burning desire, that *fiber* . . . is still the most important quality in George Brett."

Why, then, did Brett characterize himself as lackadaisical? Why did his teammates overlook his brilliance? Couldn't they see that burning desire?

"He was a little laid back," Schuerholz said. "He was a surfer from California. He gave the appearance of a relaxed, casual guy. What people didn't see was a heart as big as anyone's who's ever played in a professional uniform. He had an *aura*." Schuerholz tapped the desk top with his fingertips. "He glowed with that star quality."

Nobody noticed, apparently. Did *George* know it? (His words, *"I never thought I'd be this good,"* came back to the writer.)

"I don't think he *did* know it," Schuerholz said.

3. Comparisons

Jack Brett looked up from his crossword puzzle. "When he was seventeen and a senior in high school—" He frowned. "That's when it really struck me."

That's when baseball scouts had begun haunting the night games at Recreation Park in El Segundo, California, to watch Jack Brett's son play. "Really important people were coming to watch," he said, a teakettle hissing on the kitchen range behind him. "I went to a game one time and somebody said, 'Casey Stengel is in the stands today to see him.' Yogi Berra was there. Bobby Doerr of the Red Sox was there. Another time, Carl *Hubbell* came to see him." Jack Brett's eyes did not twinkle and he did not smile, but his voice dropped down low: "I thought, God. Maybe he's *good*."

He stared at the ponderous, leather-bound scrapbooks on the table and finally did smile, a little. "He could run so fast," he said. "When he played the outfield, scouts who saw him said they never saw him make a wrong move. They never saw him throw to the wrong base. He had a knack for playing the outfield." Jack Brett shrugged. "He was Mr. America—it was almost like he was a man among boys. I thought he could be a decathlon athlete, although I didn't know if he had the stamina. And he had a knack for doing the right thing. He was very modest. He was quiet. He was somebody you could be proud of." He looked down at a picture of his gifted son—no more than a schoolboy at the time— posing for photographers at his first World Series. "I always wanted him to play for the Yankees," the Brooklyn-born father admitted, "and I wanted him to replace Mickey Mantle."

The next day, a coach at El Segundo High School smiled when asked if Jack Brett's memory could be trusted. Really, had his son been *that* good? "There's no doubt about it," the coach said. "We haven't had any athlete go through the school who could compare with Ken Brett."

Jack Brett has a reputation for hardness—his four boys grew up chafing under his sometimes cold and demanding regime—but he is almost elegiac when he talks of his second-born, Ken. "He looked like the statue of David when he was growing up," Jack recalls. "When he was just a little boy, his stomach was so strong that you could see the plates, the muscles. Even when he was five! People used to say, 'My God, look at the development on that kid.'"

70

"With Ken, you always knew he was gonna be a star," says Bobby Brett, two years younger than Ken and two years older than George. "He wasn't just the best guy on the team. He was always the best guy in the league, by far. He was Southern California Player of the Year, two times. He was a superstar in a competitive hotbed of baseball."

The Bretts lived at 628 Penn Street in El Segundo, halfway up the hill on a narrow, tree-lined street. It's a neighborhood of modest houses with small yards nearly overgrown with shade trees, flower beds, and flowering shrubs. The Brett house was stucco with a red-brick wainscoting; brick steps led up to a wrought-iron railing and a small elevated porch. Half the facade was garage, with a short sloping driveway, too steep for basketball. A dormer window in the garage roof belonged to John—the oldest boy, who sometimes snuck out late at night and got into fights with his rowdy friends—and Ken—who did not.

The street at the top of the hill is Mariposa. From there, the Brett boys could look down on the pampered athletic fields of Recreation Park, which rests on the floor of a narrow valley—dwarfed by the spewing and flaming stacks, the pipes, and laboratorylike minarets of the Standard Oil refinery to the immediate south. El Segundo is a flowering oasis ringed by industrial giantism: to the south, the refinery; to the east, paralleling Sepulveda Boulevard, towering transmission lines; to the west, the Pacific Ocean; to the north, the gritty air and roaring runway traffic of Los Angeles International Airport. Middle class? Across the street from the baseball field, one small house shelters a tiny, immaculate lawn populated by ceramic frogs and bunnies, pink flamingos, white ducks, spread-eagled burros, painted mushrooms, and potted plants. Painted on the scoreboard in the adjoining Little League park are the words: EL SEGUNDO KIWANIS CLUB: WE BUILD. A few blocks west, El Segundo High School has expansive playing fields of its own—a football stadium and track, baseball practice fields, a scoreboard bearing the legend HOME OF THE EAGLES—and a generous, fastidiously landscaped campus dominated by imposing, symmetrical orange-brick buildings. "As you see it today," Jack Brett says, "it's not as it was before. Across from the school there are apartments now. There used to be little white frame houses, built around 1915, with narrow wood siding." One thing, though, has not changed: "The town," he says, "has a love affair with baseball."

Those who follow El Segundo baseball remember Ken Brett as the consummation of that love affair. Jack Brett's scrapbooks sparkle with the names of soon-to-be stars: basketball's Paul Westphal, football's Mike Battle and Jim Obradovich, major leaguers like Dave LaRoche, Chris Chambliss, George Brett, and his El Segundo teammate, Scott McGregor—but Ken Brett was in a class by himself. "I've never seen a kid idolized the way Ken was," Jack says. "Kemer" (his brother John couldn't pronounce "Kenneth" when he was a child) was a high-school football star till he broke his leg, played basketball for an El Segundo team that went 24-6, and struck out fourteen straight batters in a Babe Ruth League tournament game against highly rated Pasadena. In 1964, he pitched a 10-0 no-hitter over New Orleans in the Babe Ruth World Series, and not one ball was hit out

of the infield. El Segundo won the national championship that year and some observers felt that it was the
greatest Babe Ruth team ever assembled. Ken Brett hit
.462 for the series. Bobby Doerr, the Red Sox scout, said
Brett was the best prospect since the Giants Mike
McCormick twelve years before.

"I always said I'd like to be like Ken," recalls
McGregor, who went on to be a twenty-game winner for
the Baltimore Orioles. "He was an inspiration, a better
all-around athlete than me. I remember him vividly. I
watched him in Little League, in Babe Ruth, in high
school. It made the idea of pitching in the majors more
real to you. It *could* happen."

Ken Brett was on a fast track. Major league scouts bid
for his services against college coaches trumpeting the
glories of campus life. "The USC coach, Rod Dedeaux,
called all his players, 'Tiger,'" Jack Brett recalls. "I
remember one time he was with some people and he
grabs Kemer by the neck like this"—Jack makes a
tense claw of his right hand and shakes it—"and he
growls, 'He's gonna be one of our Tigers!'" Instead, Ken
signed with the Boston Red Sox, on June 23, 1966, for
$71,500 and a guarantee of eight semesters of college.
(At the signing, Ken's feet were bare under the table.
"He didn't like shoes," Jack explains.) He reported to the
Red Sox farm team in Oneonta, New York—again,
barefoot—and pitched there as "Shoeless Ken Brett." A
year later, he was the star pitcher for Pittsfield, Mas-
sachusetts, with fifteen complete games and a 1.80
earned run average, and was touted as the first good left-

hander in the Boston organization since Mel Parnell. He even got a late-season look with the Red Sox—two innings—and suddenly was inserted on the World Series roster to replace Sparky Lyle, who had a ligament sprain in his left elbow. On October 8, 1967, in St. Louis, Ken Brett walked in from the bullpen to take the mound against the Cardinals in the eighth inning of the fourth game of the World Series. With St. Louis ahead 6-0 the Red Sox looked to a miracle next day in Fenway Park. But Ken Brett enlivened the occasion. He was just nineteen—the youngest pitcher and the second youngest player to perform in the World Series (Fred Lindstrom of the New York Giants, in the 1924 Series, held the record at age eighteen and ten months). Mike Shannon was up . . . then everything sped up for the excited youngster: *Shannon, Javier* (a strikeout!), *Maxvill* (a walk), *Gibson*, and a giddy stroll to the dugout, triumphant. "Except for one walk," the *New York Times* reported the next morning, "he sent the Cardinals down more handily than the older, wiser and sadder men on the Boston staff today." The praise was echoed by his solemn teammates. "The kid really has it," admitted Carl Yastrzemski. "This boy Brett," gushed Elston Howard, "is as fast as Bob Turley was when I caught Turley in his prime with the Yankees. I also think he's as fast as Koufax was."

The Brett family was in St. Louis that day—Jack, his wife Ethel, the three Brett brothers, and Kemer's high-school coach, John Stevenson. "We went out to dinner at Stan Musial's Restaurant," Jack remembers. "We went in and there's the bats and the trophies in the cases. Kemer was dressed nicely and he said, 'Ken Brett has a reservation.' And they just ushered us past a lot of other people. I imagine it made an impression on Ken's brothers."

Indeed. Bobby Brett remembers it as though it were yesterday. "Here we are in the same lobby with George Scott and Jim Lonborg," he says, his eyes widening. "And there's our brother Ken! I said, 'Jesus Christ, I'd like to be one of those guys.'"

There was something fascinating and robust about Ken Brett's family—the dark, thin, intense accountant father with the Brooklyn accent; his tall, animated wife; and the three athletic brothers—playful, argumentative, almost boisterous. One of them—the bristly-haired fifteen-year-old—couldn't take his eyes off his baseball brother. Nine years later, the bristly-haired kid would look into a television camera at the All-Star Game in Philadelphia—this time in uniform himself. "Hi, I'm George Brett," he would say. "I'm Ken Brett's little brother."

"George was always the baby," says his mother, Ethel Johnson. (She, like Jack, has remarried.) "Everyone picked on him all the time. Which is normal, I'm sure. I feel their dad sort of favored Ken a lot. Not that he showed it, actually. But with all four of them playing baseball from Little League on to high school and American Legion ball, his dad always followed Ken more. If there were conflicting games, I always followed George." The Brett family practically lived at the ballpark during the summer: Ethel working the concession stand at Rec Park, Jack keeping score or announcing. It is remembered that they often sat on opposite sidelines at games, presumably because Jack Brett tended to smolder when his sons failed to live up to his expectation. "When you talk to Jack today," one of George's teammates reflects, "he's a class guy. But at that time we always thought he was a jerk." After a bad game, George's friends would watch their shamefaced teammate get into the car with his father, who would drive away in icy silence.

"Jack was moody," concedes McGregor. "He walked around a lot during a game. One time he'd say hi to you and the next time he'd walk right past you. He was hard on his kids, he was very intense. But my dad pushed me, too. That's the way of life in El Segundo."

"I wouldn't consider it a hard time, exactly," his mother recalls. "In Little League, if George struck out or missed a ball, his dad would get mad and yell at him. 'You should have caught that ball! You should have gotten a hit!' Things like that. He'd shrug it off later on, though."

But did George? "I hated my dad," he says flatly. "He'd say, 'Bobby wouldn't do this,' or 'Kemer wouldn't do that.' I was intimidated. I was scared to death of him." More than once, George has told this story: how he struck out twice in one game, and endured that short but painful drive up Mariposa Street with a silent, furious Jack Brett behind the wheel. "I remember I got out of the car in my uniform, my head hanging," George says, "and the next thing I felt was a foot coming right up my ass! For embarrassing the family." Brett shakes his head and smiles wanly. "That's probably where I got my hemorrhoids."

"My dad maybe treated George a little bit different," Bobby Brett ponders. "Ken was a good student, a model kid. And basically he had no problems with me; he knew

I was gonna make it. He was harder on George. George couldn't do *anything* right for him." Bobby shrugged. "But George was lazy, lacked motivation. If he hadn't made it in baseball, he *might* have had some problems. George needed somebody to get on his butt a lot."

George retorts, "Did my dad tell you about his childhood?"

"I had a good childhood," Jack Brett says very deliberately. "I had an excellent childhood. I was born in 1923, in Brooklyn. We never lacked for anything because my father always had a good job. He worked on Wall Street. He was . . . his title was 'chief clerk.' He worked on the floor of the New York Stock Exchange. He had a very responsible position and he got paid well—which at that time was forty or fifty dollars a week. That's when other people were making twenty dollars a week or not making anything at all. He had had a very hard childhood and he never wanted me or my sister to have to do what he had done—I guess he had to quit school when he was eight or nine and had to go to work. We always lived in a very nice house and my mother was never allowed to have hamburger for dinner. It was chicken or steak or roast beef or leg of lamb. He insisted on that.

"He sorta left me alone. He never wanted me to work and he always made sure I had money in my pocket. Money was, like, fifty cents." Baseball? Jack Brett chuckles. "I never made the team. I always liked the Yankees. I always hated the Dodgers.

"I read a lot. I haven't read as much in the last thirty years as I read when I was fifteen. I probably read a hundred and fifty books when I was fifteen. I didn't read any good books. I read all the Tarzan books and all the Bomba, the Jungle Boy books. I'd wake up at seven o'clock

and lay in bed till ten o'clock and read for three hours. As a consequence, I could always read, although I've read very few classics.

"I quit high school and went to work in a factory in a very large machine shop. And when I was eighteen the war came along and I joined the army, and I was in the army till 1945. I had been wounded—shot in the leg in France. They said, 'What you should do is go to school and learn something.' So I went to Pace College in New York and got a degree in business administration. Got through by the skin of my teeth.

"I got married in 1946, and began to do well as an accountant. John was born in Brooklyn. Ken, too. Bobby. But George was born in West Virginia. Two towns claim George. We really lived in Glendale, West Virginia. The next town down the road, about two miles, was Moundsville, and Moundsville had the daily newspaper. But he was really born in Glendale. . . ."

"He used to steal cars," George Brett says, sounding more amused than judgmental. "He used to get in a lot of scrapes. I think he just didn't want us to be like *him.*"

Or John.

"John was never a real good student," Ken Brett remembers. "He just liked to go out and fight. He was six-two and strong, he could clean your clock. But sometimes"—Ken grimaces, remembering the times his big brother had bit off too much and come home bruised and bleeding—"sometimes he'd just be destroyed." He shakes his head. "My father didn't like that. And *I* didn't want that."

"There's a natural pecking order in my family," Jack Brett says. "John was the king and Ken was very mild. But when John wasn't around, Ken was the king.

Whoever was the king would lord it over the others. There's a closeness between John and George because John always protected George. If he was not around and Bobby hit George, John would come home and hit Bobby. John would kick him in the rear end and say, 'Don't hit George. He's my brother and I love him.'"

"We were different kinds of families," Scott McGregor smiles. "They were pretty aggressive and we were pretty mild. We lived on a different side of town. I lived over by the ocean, across the tracks" (the poor side of town, back then). "They lived in the more affluent section." John Brett, though, seemed to be acting out a kind of working-class rebellion, emulating the pugnacious and masculine manners of the men who streamed in and out of the Standard Oil refinery gates. His best friend, football star Mike Battle, shared John's combativeness and carved out a local legend by settling crosstown rivalries with his fists. ("Mike Battle was Billy the Kid," Jack Brett remembers. "Other kids came from miles around to fight with him.") Even as adults, John and George would reply to frustration by *hitting* things . . . or people . . . smashing a batting helmet, kicking a door, poking an unwelcome photographer in the head with the tip of a crutch, breaking glass.

"John and George are very much alike," Jack Brett says. "Probably the big difference between them is that John will work very hard. Everyone that he has worked for has told me that he's a very hard worker. John's the sort who would say, 'Come on, let's get it done. Let's keep at it.' Where George would never do that. George would say, 'Let's sit down and rest for a while.'"

Comparisons like that were always being made between George and one of his brothers. But Jack Brett—

who wielded comparisons like a whip, and instilled a burning competitiveness in his sons—is not apologetic. "Maybe I neglected George," he will muse. (His son felt anything but neglected—he longed for the least respite from the paternal glare.) "I don't think I pushed him into sports so much, although I thought that would be his one salvation." Jack throws up his hands. "Because when you can't read, when you can't write . . . when you don't have those skills developed to the point of other children of the same age . . . the parent begins to say, 'Well, what the hell can this kid do?' We used to just sit there and look at him smile and say, 'Poor George.'" Jack's voice drops to a whisper. "'Poor George. What's gonna happen to him?' Cause he took shop and phys ed. Auto mechanics. No *hard* courses. Ken took four years of Spanish, four years of English, four years of biology. He would devote his time to study. Nobody had to prompt him. With George— Oh, God, it was an issue daily. It was always, 'George, did you do your homework?' And he'd say, 'I have no homework.'" Jack sniffs. "He probably didn't. He was taking shop."

Larry Cummings, the junior varsity baseball coach at El Segundo High, was also the Bretts' history teacher. "Ken was so different," he says. "I'm a tough grader and Ken got a good strong B, but Ken wasn't satisfied with a B. He repeated the course to get an A." George? Cummings smiles. "He ambled amiably through school. The teachers said, 'George—I hope you do well in baseball.'"

Jack Brett laughs. "George used to hide his report card. I'd say, 'George, where's your report card?' George would say, 'Huh? Well, uhhhh . . .' He'd put it off till tomorrow. He might be sitting with it in his pocket." Most of all, Jack Brett was alarmed by George's indifference to the written word. "He didn't *wanta* read. Bobby used to read the newspaper. On Saturday mornings when I got up, Bobby would be reading the sports pages and he'd read me the article out of the paper. If you tried to get *George* to read the articles—" He laughs again. "—it was *discouraging* to hear."

Jack Brett shrugs. "Of course, I hear him talk now and I'm very proud of him. He was a late bloomer. His baseball skills developed continuously . . . and so did his mind. I think he's very honest. Very open." Jack looks thoughtful. "He doesn't hold back."

No, George Brett does not hold back. One afternoon, at the Royals training camp in Fort Myers, Brett leaned back in his reclining chair in the clubhouse and recalled how his father's perfectionism had haunted him into adulthood. "I called him up once from New York," George said, staring up at the ceiling in an unconscious parody of the psychoanalytic posture. "My brother was with the Pirates then, playing a doubleheader in San Diego. And I think Kemer won the first game and got a hit. Then he tripled off the wall in the second game. So my dad said, 'Get any hits today?' I said, 'No.' He says, 'George, your brother is a *pitcher* and he's outhitting you.' And he started screaming at me on the phone." George made a face. "I just hung up the phone. Then I threw the phone against the wall, tore it out of the wall. I went and slugged the full-length mirror. Shattered it! Threw a chair against the wall. [Royals catcher] Buck Martinez was my roommate then, and poor Buck didn't know what to say." George shook his head. "He made *constant* comparisons," he said bitterly. "I was not as good as my brothers. I *never* would be as good as my brothers."

Back in El Segundo, coach John Stevenson smiles knowingly when he hears such stories about Jack Brett. Stevenson's hair is fading from blond to white now—he was a young baseball coach when John Brett captained his El Segundo team—and he walks with the upright bearing of the veteran baseball man. He would look as comfortable managing the Yankees as he does his perennial prep champion teams. "I think there was fear of wasting their talents," Stevenson said one spring night in the upstairs office behind home plate at Recreation Park. "I can tell you—he really loved those kids." The scourges of drugs and alienation had begun to frighten parents in the late sixties, and El Segundo, despite its physical isolation, its Shangri-La quality, suffered the same generational conflict that racked the nation. "I remember Jack called up Kemer once after seeing him on TV. He said," Stevenson spoke sharply, squinting, "'Cut your hair!'" He leaned back in his chair, smiling. "Have you noticed Jack's appearance? Shoes always shined? Clothes always right?" He laughed and shook his head. "George used to drive him crazy. T-shirt, shoes with no socks."

Both Stevenson and Jack Brett remember, with some amusement, their first meeting. It was a near argument, precipitated when the coach disciplined John Brett one day by ordering him to sit alone on the team bus through a double-header. After showering, Stevenson came out to be greeted by an angry father. "There's Jack standing there, leaning against the bus," Stevenson remembers, "and I said, 'Wanta talk?'" Stevenson recalls Jack

Brett's stern, indignant response: "He said, 'I've *always* got time to talk when it pertains to my kids.'"

Stevenson may have seen glimpses of himself in Jack Brett. "John was hard, too," McGregor says. "He got married late, and for a long time he lived his life for the team. He's a lot like Earl [Weaver, manager of the Orioles]. He demanded a lot from us and you didn't get a lot of praise. He'd get on you good. He wasn't accepted in El Segundo at first because he was so hard." Time, though, smoothed over many resentments. The El Segundo Eagles troop back loyally every year for the Alumni Baseball Game. Even the major leaguers come back, when they can, to throw batting practice for Stevenson or to coach his wide-eyed youngsters. "The school has always been there for us," McGregor says. "We love it. John just milks us, keeps asking questions to help his kids." Parents long ago stopped questioning the efficacy of Stevenson's methods. "They've had two good basketball teams in the last twenty years," Jack Brett says. "But in the last twenty years they've had *twenty* good baseball teams."

Success, they say, breeds success. When the high-school team plays at night at Rec Park, the little brothers of the varsity players romp in the half-light on the neighboring grass of the Little League field—chasing foul balls, tackling each other, playing catch with oversized gloves. John Stevenson watched all four Brett boys chase around like that, yelling shrilly and laughing, punching and wrestling with each other till the tears came. "I knew George when he was eight years old," he said. "I'd watch him runnin' around the park here, swingin' the bat. They used to call him 'Lou.' When he came in as a ninth grader, he was only five-one and a hundred and five pounds. The JV coach back then had a team of eleventh graders and he wanted to cut George. I said, 'You can't cut him.' He said, 'He's just so *small.'* But the next year, George started on the varsity." Stevenson nods. "John was exactly the same. As a ninth grader he was tiny, and as an eleventh grader he was a *hulk.*"

Since George Brett had almost been cut from his high-school team (the story has made the rounds in magazine articles, with George gaining about five pounds per article until he is remembered as a roly-poly kid), outsiders seized on the notion that Brett was a mediocre player. Which made it hard to explain why the Royals had drafted him in the second round of the 1971 free-agent draft, or how the ambidextrous youngster, as a senior, had been allowed to play every position in a prep all-star game, climaxed by a ninth inning in which he pitched both right-handed and left-handed and retired the side. "I thought George was the third-best player on his team." Bobby Brett says, naming Scott McGregor as the obvious standout. Six players from George's 1971 high-school team, which went 33-2, went on to play pro ball, and McGregor, who had long been the attention getter, had pitched their Babe Ruth team to a second World Series championship. "The highest George ever hit in high school was about .340," Bobby says. "Which isn't great for high school." Jack Brett, when asked if he suspected back then that his youngest son would one day be a star, answers quickly, "Oh, no. Not at all."

Stevenson disagrees, "He was a *great* player. He *wasn't* mediocre. That's bullshit. George was an outstanding shortstop, a super hitter and a great all-around performer. I saw him play his first year up at Billings [then the Royals rookie farm club]. He was a superplayer there too."

But even Stevenson has to admit, "He wasn't as *intense* a player as he is now."

Jack Brett smiles at that one. "Kemer was probably a *hundred* times more intense," he recalls. "Before a game, he would become almost morose. He wouldn't sit for six hours in a trance, but he'd drift off, thinking about the game. George? George would be thinking about going down to the beach. Baseball was just something to do because all the other guys were doing it." Of course, when it came to intensity, even Kemer was an also-ran in the Brett family. "John had more desire than any of us," George concedes. "He *loved* it."

Yes, George played the comparison game too. Comparisons were unavoidable, Jack Brett points out, even if he hadn't used them to manipulate his sons. As he puts it, "If George wasn't eager, he was compared to John. If he wasn't smart, he was compared to Bobby. And if he wasn't smooth, he was compared to Kemer." George Brett couldn't escape evaluation even when his brothers had finally graduated and he was king of his own kingdom of one. Before the 1971 season, coach Stevenson had his talented team take marking pencils to a 110-question personality inventory. "It was designed to measure qualities like aggressiveness," Stevenson recalls, "mental toughness." And how had the computer pegged young George Brett? Stevenson smiles and says, "He was sort of the con-man type"—the type of player, in other words, who would not respond well to praise. (Or, as Brett remembers it, "Never give the SOB any credit or he'll start doggin' it.") The rest of the year, Stevenson withheld the usual praise from his talented shortstop. According to Jack Brett, "George would be broken-hearted because the coach never gave him an accolade. He'd have a good game and come home saying, 'He wouldn't say a word to me! Other guys—he says how great *they* are!'" George Brett was baffled and hurt. "I pretty much left him alone," Stevenson says, pointing out that while he was loath to praise George, he didn't yell at the youngest Brett either. "I figured he got enough of that at home."

Ken Brett buttoned up his Hawaiian shirt in the deserted Royals clubhouse at Fort Myers, smiling at Bobby Brett's memory of him as a nineteen-year-old World Series hero—a titan with fancy cars, beautiful girls at his elbow, money in his pocket. "Twenty dollars was a lot in those days," Ken said. His smile widened. "He didn't tell you that ten days later I was in the army and they forgot all about me!" He slipped his feet into a pair of sandals. "That was a humbling experience. Those guys in the army didn't care about the World Series. They wanted me in the kitchen with a shovel in my hand."

No army could have taken Ken Brett on a lengthier odyssey than had baseball. It was his fourteenth major league season and the Royals were his tenth major league club. He had figured in trades involving twenty-three players and had been signed three times as a free agent. He sometimes sat by himself in the clubhouse with a vacant—or reflective—look on his face, in the manner of veteran pitchers who have wasted too many days of their lives waiting for their next turn. But he looked no older than his famous younger brother, and a copy of *Architectural Digest* in his locker suggested that his travels had not put his mind to sleep. In big cities, he was known to favor the art galleries of a morning, and those who looked past the strong family resemblance— he had been mistaken for, and interviewed as, George during the .400 frenzy—noted features slightly softer and a manner more reserved and introspective.

"I went right to spring training and started throwing the ball too hard," he said, recalling his return to civilian life in 1968. "I was young, trying to impress people. I wanted to stay with the Red Sox. But I wound up in Triple A and pitched eight innings the first time out." He shook his head ruefully. "I shoulda known better." In his second outing, Ken had lasted seven innings. "The next time"—he smiled—"I couldn't throw twenty feet." (Jack Brett remembers visiting Kemer that winter at Fort Ord, California. "I said, 'When you get down there, *don't* try to catch up.' And dammit, two weeks later he was down there and pitching opening day.")

"I don't think that would happen now," Ken said, observing baseball's current solicitude for young arms. He pitched only twenty-nine innings for Louisville in 1968, and forever after his left elbow would plague him in fits and starts, through surgery in 1974, when his arm was locked in a bent position (major league pitcher and surgical resident Doc Medich assisted), through drug therapy, chiropractic, and finally acupuncture. He would never win more than 13 games in a season (he was 13-9 in consecutive seasons for Philadelphia and Pittsburgh), but when the pain abated he showed the stuff that had inflamed the scouts: 155 strikeouts in 139 innings for the 1970 Red Sox; winning pitcher for the National League in the 1974 All-Star Game; 16 complete games and a 3.31 ERA for the 1976 Chicago White Sox. Still, it was hard not to think of his career as wasted. The emergence of George Brett as a great hitter was a poignant footnote to the career of Ken, who, as a pitcher, had logged only 347 at bats in his career. The figures were tantalizing: a .262 batting average (despite the fact that everyday players shooed pitchers out of the batting cage), 18 doubles, 10 home runs, 44 runs batted in. Ken Brett held just one major league record for a pitcher, and it was for *hitting:* he had once blasted home runs in four consecutive games.

"I asked him one time," Jack Brett says, "when he was twenty-one and wasn't doing too well. I said, 'Ken, why don't you tell 'em you want to play the outfield?' And he said, 'I'd have to go back to the minors and start over again.'" Jack pauses. "I asked him again, much later, and he said, 'It's my pride now. I want to do well as a pitcher.'"

"I don't think he ever felt it was his decision," John Stevenson counters. "Ken's still pitching 'cause he *loves* it. He doesn't need it. He's made a good deal of money in baseball and invested it wisely. He can probably walk away from baseball and never miss it."

Ken Brett checked his pockets for his keys and wallet. "I think you can ask any older player. The older they get, the more they enjoy the game." He looked too young to talk that way, but it was true. For Ken Brett, just shagging balls in the outfield and pitching batting practice were pleasures borrowed against time. He looked thoughtful. "It probably borders on love."

George Brett stuck his head in the door, his hair matted with sweat, "You leaving now, Kemer?" Ken nodded. "Don't go yet," George said, and disappeared into the sunshine.

Ken Brett smoothed his hair back and put on a bemused smile. "I look in the mirror sometimes and say, 'I'm thirty-two years old and I've never worked a day in my life.'"

The vista from Bobby Brett's office window is one of blue ocean and a curve of rocky coastline sweeping north and west from Hermosa Beach, California—some of the most expensive real estate in the world. He dresses casually, talks briskly, and sprinkles his business calls with the dialogue of screenplay wheeler-dealers: "He came in fair . . . a million-one, a million-two . . . what's the asking? . . ." Bobby manages the financial holdings of George and Ken Brett, surrounded by young and attractive associates who dress well, live well, and know how to deal. But he made his own fortune first. "I didn't know what I was doing," he smiles, revealing the distinctive Brett gap in his front teeth (George has had his capped). "I started in real estate in the summer of 1975, and I went in cold turkey." His own bid for baseball stardom had stalled at the A level in the Royals organization, where he couldn't see wasting a decade in dimly lighted ballparks and creaking buses. "I said, 'If I don't move up a league every year, I better hang it up.' They had guys that were younger than me, who were bigger, stronger, faster"—his eyebrows shoot up—"*and* got money to sign." He shrugs. "It wasn't the end of the world."

Bobby taught for a year at a predominantly black high school—"I envisioned myself as a coach"—but had suffered from classroom frustration and outside harassment, such as sugar in his car's gas tank. "I wasn't really qualified to do anything," he confesses. So he had turned to real estate. In a few short years, he had traded in his old car for a Mercedes, his old digs for a $350,000 condominium on the beach, and his old—well, he would trade almost anything.

"It was originally Ken and I," he says, relaxing at home. His arms are draped on the back of a modular couch; sunlight streams in through the sliding doors to his sun deck. "Then it was one third each, with George in it." He waves his hand to take in the building, including Ken's condo next door. "This little piece of sand is worth nine hundred thousand dollars."

Bobby Brett lives in the present tense.

The temptation with Ken Brett or George—with any ballplayer—is to dwell on their grand and poignant moments, to apply the sepia tones of myth to their still young lives.

Bobby Brett won't stand for that. "Do you know where he is right now?" Ken said in April, 1981. "He's in Philadelphia at the NCAA basketball finals, and he has no ticket. But I guarantee you—tonight he'll be on the court somewhere. And he won't spend a *penny*."

"Bobby is a salesman," George said, signifying by a stern look that this was an understatement. "He's always making deals. His great line is, 'Look, if *you* don't buy it, I will. I'm giving you the first chance.'"

Ken laughed. "He's the only one my parents put through college."

"Bobby's very well organized," Jack Brett says. "When he was thirteen, he would allocate his time—to basketball or baseball, to football, to study. One Saturday morning, while we were waiting for breakfast, we were sitting there and he was diagraming football plays. And I said, 'What are you doing, Bob?' And he said, 'I'm diagraming football plays.' And I said, 'Well, don't you know them all?' And he said, 'I'm diagraming every guy's assignment.' That's the way he approached sports. Bobby's a recognized leader."

Bobby's friends remember him as a brash child, capable of insinuating himself into any desired position. If he bought seats to see the Los Angeles Lakers at the Forum, he inevitably ended up at court side. If he went to Dodger Stadium with his dad and brothers, he somehow lied his way into the press box and copped free food and press handouts. "I was aggressive enough to go up to people," he says. "When the Angels played at Wrigley Field once, I saw Steve Bilko over by the screen. I said, 'Hey, Steve!' but he was talking to some other people. But I just kept at him and kept at him until he finally gave in and gave me an autograph.

"I was probably a pain in the ass," Bobby mutters.

"There's some tension," observes Clint Hurdle. "Have you met little Kemer, John's kid? He'll send him out to live with George for a week or so. So George starts telling John how to run his life. He says, You're terrible, you're terrible, you're in the streets, you're *nothing.* . . ."

Hurdle looks amazed. "This is his older brother! This guy's *huge,* he's beat him up a couple of times!"

"John's the craziest," says catcher Jamie Quirk, Brett's Royals teammate and best friend. Quirk remembers a night in 1974 when some of the Brett tension spilled over on the sidewalk in front of an El Segundo bar. "It was the night before Thanksgiving and we were all out in George's area, where they grew up. We were out drinking, you know? We started pretty early in the afternoon, so it was only about eight o'clock at night. George went out to make a call at a pay phone right outside the bar, and his brother Johnny said, 'What are you doing? Where are you going?'

"George said, 'I'm gonna call up this girl.' So he goes out. And Johnny didn't like it, or something like that. He thought George was gonna be leaving us and goin' with some chick and he'd be left alone drinking. So it ended up in heated words and they actually started fighting." Quirk smiles. "I tried to break it up, and I probably got beat up worse than those two."

John Brett's fights, according to his brothers, are not the type that end in a couple of glancing haymakers and a muttered apology. The El Segundo police, on this occasion, were summoned to corral the flailing and grunting brothers and haul the whole bunch to jail. "They put Johnny in one cell and George in another," Quirk says, "while the cops asked *me* all the questions. So I call up the other brother, Bobby, and Bobby comes down to the El Segundo jail. This is like half an hour later.

"They go, 'Okay, we're gonna release *one* of them. Which one do you want?'

"We go, 'Okay, give us George.'" Quirk begins to laugh. "And John is in the other cell goin' crazy, he's ready to kill Bobby, ready to kill George, he's ready to kill *me*."

George remembers. "They wanted to let us out one hour apart," he says cheerfully. "We were in separate cells, but John was gonna bend the bars to get at me." The next day, when John arrived for the family's Thanksgiving dinner, George began shadowboxing, taunting his older brother. "I said, 'Come on—you're going *down*!'" He laughs. "That's John's expression— 'You're going *down*!'"

"They've been that way their whole life," Quirk says. "They can be real crude to each other, real crude."

"John hasn't changed very much," Jack Brett says. "When he was young, he thought he could rule the roost. He *still* feels that way; he's the oldest brother. He's big and strong. He feels that the others should listen to him."

"John was very feisty," his mother agrees. "He always had a chip on his shoulder. He still does. And boy, don't let anybody touch any of his brothers, or say anything bad about them! He's very protective." It seemed unfortunate, to those who knew him, that John Brett could not channel his aggressiveness in professional athletics. ("I could be totally wrong," Jamie Quirk says, "but I think John's a little frustrated that he never stayed with baseball.") His baseball career ended at the A level in the Red Sox system—shortened by injury, a teenage marriage, and the responsibilities of raising an infant son. His best friend, Mike Battle, wound up as a wild-man kick-return specialist for the New York Jets in the late sixties—a workingman's folk hero, throwing elbows and straight-arms, bloodying noses, lunging into bone-crunching tackles on the dead run. Back home, John Brett hammered nails on construction projects. Football validated Mike Battle's brawling tendencies; the El Segundo police attended to John's.

"It's very hard to say why John's different," George says. "He has different ideas of fun." George is still the closest to John; Bobby and Ken imply a distance from their oldest brother that borders on alienation. George sees that distance as a consequence of John's occupation as a framing contractor. "He's married, he's got a wife and kids. He has obligations. He works from six A.M. till four P.M., and he's tired. But *we*" (the other three, independent brothers who maintain a vacation retreat on a Palm Springs golf course), "we can do anything we want. Go wherever we want. We'll say, 'Let's go to Las Vegas this afternoon.'" George looks frustrated. "But John *can't*. He thinks, 'The sons a bitches are going to Palm Springs for the weekend!' It's difficult to accept that."

Or maybe it was a disturbance in the family pecking order, dating back to when John Brett was the captain of his high-school baseball team—and his little brother was the star. "Kemer was a little divisive within the family," coach Stevenson says. "He was so good that you could see he was going to be a major league player. John was immediately known as Kemer's big brother, and it drove him crazy. It would come out if John had a bad day."

"It wasn't like George ever stole *my* spotlight," Bobby Brett says, "but Ken stole the spotlight from John." He shrugs. "And John didn't handle it too well."

The pecking order—with the Bretts it was more punching than pecking—appeals to Jack Brett's sense of order, if not to his sense of decorum. He doesn't deny that he has always felt closest to Ken in his glory moments. "Yeah, 'cause Ken has been much more—" He hesitates. "Ken is a very gentle guy inside. He's very considerate. Ken is the most considerate guy in the world. Bobby a little less so . . . George a little less . . . and John a little less. That's the sequence." He struggles for an example. "Ken is the kind of guy who will call me up and say, 'I haven't taken you out to dinner for a couple of weeks, let's go to dinner.' Or, 'What time's dinner? I'm comin' over.'

"Bobby will do that occasionally." Jack smiles. "Ken does it because he feels that's the thing to do. Bobby does it because it's a *meal*." Jack chuckles. "It's a meal and 'I like to see my dad.'

"George will do it if the others are there. Then *he'll* come. . . .

"And John will never do it."

Ken Brett can smile at his dad's comparisons. "We put him through the wringer," he says. "We were always at each other's throats."

The smile derives from the impression, shared by all the Brett brothers, that their father has changed. "He's really mellowed out," George admits. "I don't know what made him change so much. Possibly the divorce? Maybe my success had something to do with it."

"Sometimes I think he's a little narrow," Ken adds,

"but he's getting better. Now you can argue with him a little bit." He smiles again at the thought. *The will of steel finally bends, the father finally relaxes his grip.* "You can't change the world by yourself," Ken says.

Jack Brett sees it as a natural cycle common to families. "When they get to be fourteen or fifteen, they think their parents are terrible," he says. "They *love* them . . . but they wish their parents wouldn't do the things they do, like try to make them study or yell at them when the report card comes home. But as they grow older . . ." He sighs. "I think they come back to the parents again. When they *really* become adults. Then they come back to the family." That philosophy, he says, sustains him now that his children are grown, their glories captured in his overflowing scrapbooks. He does not feel a deep hurt, he says, at the sometimes jaundiced eye with which they review his parenting; he does not begrudge them their independence. "There'll always be a closeness," he says. "I really believe that the parent should not intrude on the children's lives. Naturally, I wish they'd call me up every day—but I don't call *my* mother every day, so I understand." His voice turns wistful again. "I'm glad to be around them. I enjoy just standing there and looking at them. Not only from pride, but the closeness and the love." He smiles. "I've done that. I've been to parties and they'll be sitting down, the four of them, laughing and talking and having a great time. And I'll just stand off ten feet and look at them and just say, 'Isn't that great . . . that they're such good friends?'

"But to go over and try to join in with them . . ."

His voice trails off.

*   *   *

Finally we have a baseball game with these grown men. They play again, as in childhood, at Recreation Park in El Segundo. The red light still blinks atop the El Segundo water tower; the refinery stacks are lit up like a carnival. Little kids chase each other around on the Little League field. Heavy jets roar aloft over the trees on the left-field embankment (Bobby Brett remembers the day, years ago, when a small plane crashed near the field). Several thousand neighbors and friends (and fans) pack the bleachers and press against the chain link fence that surrounds the outfield.

George Brett and Scott McGregor play for the team of the seventies; Ken Brett for the team of the sixties, with brother Bobby (they gave him sergeant's stripes for Christmas) as player-manager. Many of the players are heavy-bellied and slow, but they play with joy and abandon. "Jim Obradovich's dad umpired," coach Stevenson laughs. "George went after him after one call, nose to nose, like Earl Weaver. Everybody just loved it."

Youth prevails: the seventies wins the game, 9-8, with George Brett batting "five guys out of turn" in the final inning to assure victory. But *Kemer* Brett is the Most Valuable Player. "The bat feels like a foreign object in my hands," he jokes, but hasn't he just socked two home runs off twenty-game winner McGregor? "I hit two in every alumni game," Ken says. "It's getting to be automatic." He adds, "You don't have to hit it real hard here to put it out."

George Brett, too, has homered, a blast, McGregor jokes, that "almost took out a row of trees in center field." But it's not quite like the major leagues, where

"I NEVER THOUGHT I'D BE THIS GOOD"

George's exploits earn him silver bats and Player of the Year trophies. This is *home*. "Kemer deserved the MVP," George acknowledges. "My brother Bobby deserved the Worst Manager. He took my brother out to soon."

The needling of Bobby is deserved. George almost sputters as he describes the fraternal treachery. "Bobby wanted to show me up. Or Kemer. He intentionally walked a right-handed hitter to face *me* with the bases loaded. *Then*—" he smiles knowingly, "he brings Kemer in to pitch to me."

How many managers had played the percentages the *other* way in Brett's .390 season? How many had said, like Detroit's manager Sparky Anderson, "Brett will never beat me. He'll get walked"?

"What annoyed me," George says mischievously, "is that the people were rooting for Kemer!" He shakes his head ruefully. "He's still bigger than me in El Segundo."

George grounded out.

PART TWO

THE ROYALS TRIANGLE

1. The Eagle Flies on Friday

"Coaches in the past were used too much as mechanical people," said John Wathan. "Just throwing batting practice, just hitting ground balls, just coaching bases." The stereotype was familiar: the baseball coach as beer-bellied buffoon, promoting false hustle, clapping his hands and barking, "Little chatter out there!" swapping lies and cash at all-night poker sessions with the manager and the traveling secretary. "But you think of the coach in high school, college, or the minor leagues," Wathan continued, "as an *instructor.*"

The Royals, in 1973, had a coach on their roster who was called just that: batting instructor.

Instructor.

On another club that title would have prompted guffaws. Hitting a baseball was considered a mystical business, tampered with at great risk to a ballplayer's "talent"—and only then in the gravest of emergencies, such as a prolonged and desperate slump. The Royals, however—as evidenced by their bold and costly experiment, the Royals Baseball Academy—believed that even the gifted athlete could be taught something and the marginal player *had* to be. It was a philosophy which this particular coach, Charley Lau, embraced unreservedly. "As long as baseball is played," he has said, "there will be people who believe you throw bats and balls on the field and play—the strong or the talented will survive. And then there's the other side, that says, 'Hey, they need proper guidance to get started in the right direction.'" Charley Lau belongs to the second school.

George Brett was twenty years, two months, and eighteen days old on August 2, 1973, when he played his first major league ball game. He was, at the time, the youngest Royal ever, an emergency replacement for injured third baseman Paul Schaal, and although he was a solid prospect, based on not quite three minor league seasons, Brett could not yet survive a test against the strong and talented of the big leagues. His best batting average was a .291 for Billings, Montana, in 1971. His glove was suspect, his throwing arm was wild, he was an unaggressive base runner, and scouts questioned his ability to keep his weight down. In forty at bats for the Royals, Brett managed only five base hits for a .125 average, drove in no runs. The rookie, who had set a five-year deadline for making the major leagues, had reached the majors, all right—due to Schaal's misfortune—but he had definitely not *made* it. And yet—despite Brett's sorry statistics and obvious lack of direction—Charley Lau, the coach, the *instructor,* offered little tangible

102

advice. He threw the struggling rookie out on the field with the bats and balls. "I have a philosophy," Lau said later, "that you let people be, for the first year or so. Unless there's a glaring fault in the swing." Convinced by this lack of attention that his first visit to the majors would be a short one, Brett kept his suitcases close at hand, and waited for the phone call from upstairs that would dispatch him back to the Nebraska farm club, the Omaha Royals. In the meantime, he absorbed the sights and sounds of the big leagues, not altogether confident that he would be back soon.

Nineteen seventy-three was an exciting year for Kansas City baseball. The Royals finished second in the West, only six games behind the Oakland A's; they won the most games in Kansas City's major league history, 88; and they drew 600,000 more fans than the year before, 1,345,341. The Royals had established stars, like Gold Glove center fielder Amos Otis, slugging first baseman John Mayberry, and All-Star second baseman Cookie Rojas, like Paul Splittorff and Rookie of the Year pitcher Steve Busby (who had thrown a no-hitter in April). For the first time, the expansion Royals were seen as a genuine threat to the star-laden A's. "The Royals need just one more starting pitcher," it was said, or, "A little right-handed power and they'll catch the A's," or, "If [pitcher] Rollie Fingers gets a hangnail, the A's will fall back in the pack." The Royals—long poised on the brink of respectability—were suddenly getting respect.

But even a winning team harbors failure and disappointment somewhere on the roster. The player who would later stand out in Brett's memory was a twenty-seven-year-old outfielder the Royals had acquired from the Cincinnati Reds in a winter deal. Although used by the Reds primarily as a pinch hitter, this player had performed well in the 1972 World Series. He had some power in his bat, too, and had picked up a few reckless baserunning habits from a fiery college coach and an equally feisty minor league manager named Don Zimmer. Unfortunately, this proud player had come to the junior circuit with expectations of instant success. He planned, in his own words, to "feast" on the American League's supposedly inferior pitching, which was dominated, he had heard, by weak-armed hurlers who stooped to trickery and location pitching to get batters out. (In the National League, pitchers took a perverse pride in throwing to a batter's strength. They called it "challenging" the hitters.)

"I kinda got a rude awakening," he would say later. American League pitchers, knowing that this player had built his reputation by scalping pitches on the inside corner of the plate, threw the frustrated newcomer everything *but* the inside fastball. Low screwballs. Outside curves. Lazy change-ups, too high to hit. A .278 hitter the year before, this player's batting average began to drop like the thermometer in January. He expressed his frustration in the classic manner—throwing his helmet, flinging his bat, battering the water cooler.

Charley Lau—just as he would later with George Brett—seemed at first to view the disintegration of this new Royal dispassionately. "Charley's not the sort of guy that would volunteer a lot of information," Wathan recalls. "You had to drag it out of him." In the absence of that prodding, Lau did not force himself on the young man, but neither did he accept the outfielder's confident claim that he would soon break out of the slump. "No," Lau said, "you may be a good hitter, but you're not gonna hit like that." He shook his head slowly. "The way you're doin' things mechanically at the plate, it's not gonna happen."

"Yes, it will," the player insisted. "I always hit like this." But his average fell below .200. Yanked for a pinch hitter in a game against the Texas Rangers, the outfielder pinwheeled from explosive fury to deep anguish. He kicked. He groaned. He was benched.

Lau watched and waited. "A player has to find out if he can do it his way," he explains. "Or *any* way. Then, if it doesn't work, he's very dedicated. He's *anxious* to learn." This player finally reached that point. Defeated. Humbled. "I can remember," Lau says, "he was hitting .188 when he finally came to me and said, 'Okay, let's talk.'"

Lau, a man of few words, replied, "Wait till you get to .180."

The player's name was Hal McRae.

"I rebelled the first half of 1973," McRae recalls. "I was headstrong. But I think that's good. You have to have enough confidence in yourself to say, 'I can do it by myself.'" He smiled. "But then, at some point you've gotta be sensible enough to say, 'Maybe I can't. Maybe I need a little help.'" McRae admits that he waited too long. "I was hitting .188!" he laughs. "I finally went to Charley and said, 'Forget everything I said. Here I am! Do what you want with me. *Anything!*' He coulda told me to try standing on one foot, put the bat between my legs, and flick it with my thighs, and I would've tried it."

Lau's advice was not that radical, but his hitting theories did depart from prevailing baseball wisdom. He worshiped consistency. He believed that a player producing eight singles a week would win more games for the Royals than a player hitting four home runs a month. There were, to be sure, other baseball men who shared this viewpoint, but few who had had success convincing impatient young hitters. For years, free-swinging sluggers and marginal power hitters alike had tried to pull the ball, aiming for the closer fences, "guessing" pitches in hopes of meeting the ball in front of the plate, flailing out of rhythm with stride and stroke. The 20-home-run hitter with a .203 average and 82 strikeouts stalked the majors. It was as if pro basketball players shot only eighty-foot hook shots, demanding superstar salaries because twelve or thirteen a season lucked in. McRae, humbling himself before Lau, was asking how to shoot lay-ups. "I'm not gonna say Hal was a dummy," Lau recalls; "he was just an ordinary dumb *hitter*. He was aware of one pitch and was successful with it in the National League, but there was a different philosophy in the American League and he didn't see it over here. The harder he tried the worse he got."

The lessons were held most afternoons in the batting cage at Royals Stadium an hour or so before regular batting practice. Players working with Lau generally wore T-shirts and went hatless, but the ball boys shagging in the outfield wore full Royals uniforms, sweat streaking their young faces. Lau, or another coach, would throw pitch after pitch to McRae from behind a protective screen, reloading from a super-market shopping cart filled with baseballs, till the bat was slippery in McRae's hands and the sweat ran into his eyes. For some players, the cage wasn't big enough to contain their frustrations—"It doesn't feel comfortable," was the average ballplayer's response to any change in his swing—but McRae turned out to be a cheerful and diligent pupil. He learned to "go with the pitch"—that is, to hit the outside pitch hard to right field instead of trying to steer it to left. Lau told him to back off the plate and square up his stance. He said to stop trying to outguess the pitchers. He had McRae shorten his swing, develop a rhythmic plate ritual, hit *down* on the ball instead of up, and told him to try to hammer every pitch right back into the pitcher's belly. McRae followed orders, and the result, when executed properly, was usually a line drive. But McRae also spent hours by himself practicing his stroke on a hitting tee—hitting the ball against an outfield wall, retrieving it, teeing up, and hitting it again. The improvement was gradual but marked, and when he broke out of his slump, hitting two home runs in one game, McRae's exultation was as pronounced as his previous depression had been. "He just went crazy," Brett recalls. "I mean, he was the drunkest guy I'd ever seen, squirting fire extinguishers in the hallway and drop-kicking doors. I was rooming with [outfielder] Tom Poquette then, and Mac kicked our door in. Pokey called the police 'cause he didn't know who it was." By season's end, McRae had lifted his average to an inglorious but improved .234 with 9 home runs and 50 RBIs, and he credited the return of his confidence and his skill entirely to Charley Lau. "He was very patient and understanding," McRae recalls. "A lot of coaches give the people that are going *well* all the attention, but it's when things are goin' *bad* that you need understanding and attention. That's what Charley did with me."

Under Lau's tutelage, McRae hit .310 in 1974 and .295 over the next eight American League seasons: he became the preeminent designated hitter in the American League—a hitting specialist whose career was fragmented into disjointed plate appearances and brief, wild forays onto the base paths. But his world was less that of the open sky and wind-whipped pennants and more that of the tunnel behind the Royals dugout, where he exercised and sprinted during games to keep loose for his times at bat. The tunnel was a cold, clammy passage, even in late summer, lit by wire-caged bulbs in the ceiling. It was regularly washed down with a garden hose, making the walls sweat and the green carpet runner erupt in ugly pustules that the ground crew periodically lanced, trimmed, and reglued. Jean Valjean, splashing through the sewers of Paris, was the model for Hal McRae in the big leagues.

It wasn't that McRae *couldn't* play the outfield. He was adequate. It was rather that Whitey Herzog, alarmed at McRae's habit of running into walls and diving on the asphalt-hard turf, thought him too valuable a hitter to risk outfield injury. "Mac plays the game like everybody played it twenty-five years ago," Herzog said one day. He looked wistful, remembering, perhaps, St. Louis's Gashouse Gang, baserunning terrorists who came in with spikes high and sent infielders tumbling. "The game's become a *gentleman*'s game," Herzog said.

"You're not supposed to throw at people anymore, you're not supposed to take 'em out on the double play. But to me, that's just the way the game should be played." Herzog shrugged. Having Hal McRae in the tunnel was like having a bottle of Chateau Lafite 1806 in the wine cellar.

Sometimes, Herzog praised his DH by saying, "Mac's more a ballplayer from the old school"—that is, before the era of batting helmets batting gloves, and clubhouse hair dryers. But the old school had been closed for years, and some managers around the league were less nostalgic. They squawked when McRae took out a shortstop by sliding fourteen feet to the right of second base . . . or *didn't* slide and rollblocked the pivot man into center field. His home plate collisions were legendary, football-like crashes that lifted a catcher off his feet, raised a huge cloud of dust, and left the ball spinning on the ground. Once, when McRae's attempted home-plate annihilation of former teammate Bob Stinson left an eight-inch gash in the catcher's hand, the then Seattle manager Darrell Johnson called the play "the dirtiest I've seen in fifteen years."

McRae's response? "I think a lot of players now just want to be friends with everybody." He smiled meekly. "But I've sorta been an aggressive person all my life. Plus, I was *taught* to play like that. It was my college coach's philosophy at Florida A & M. He wanted you to be the intimidator and not be intimidated. I think it's part of the game, and my only purpose is to help the club win." He hesitated. "I guess *everybody* would like to be liked . . . but I won't compromise to be liked."

To young George Brett, getting his first sniff of the big

leagues, Hal McRae's example was revelatory. Why this should be so no one can explain—Brett was well coached as a youngster, and fiery play is given lip service at every level of baseball—but something in McRae's bone-jarring, reckless style caught his fancy. "Once I saw how he was sliding," Brett recalls, "the way he ran the bases . . . well, I saw second basemen get a little intimidated. I saw shortstops get intimidated. I saw him take the extra base on outfielders. And I thought"—Brett's face assumes the glow of revelation—"if we get *three* or *four* guys on the ball club doing that, it would tremendously help our chances to win."

Although Brett's explanation is not entirely satisfying—resolutions to alter one's temperament in the interest of self-improvement are usually just wishful thinking—a metamorphosis began. Brett opened the 1974 season with the Omaha Royals, but after sixteen games the parent club traded Paul Schaal to the Angels and brought Brett back up to the majors. He began to emulate Hal McRae, sliding ferociously, challenging outfielders, dirtying his uniform. "He used to be so lackadaisical," Bobby Brett marveled. "If he got one or two hits he was happy. But now, if he got three, he wanted *four*. His concentration is just fantastic, and he's such a competitor. He wants to *beat* you." Of course, aggressiveness alone could not stretch singles into doubles. A measure of baseball wisdom was required: the ability to judge how quickly an outfielder could make a throw if fielding the ball across his body, a knowledge of throwing arms, an instinct for situations, an awareness of field conditions like wet grass and soft spots. George Brett, like some sleepy-eyed creature just wakening to the world around him, greedily absorbed this minutiae, seeking a competitive edge; and often, he looked to Hal McRae. Before long, despite only average speed, Brett, too, owned a reputation as one of the best base runners in baseball. "I've never seen anybody make so many doubles out of hard grounders to dead center field," a teammate praised. "His instincts are incredible."

Instincts? Brett would shrug and say, "I got it from McRae."

One afternoon, a few years after the McRae revelations changed his game, Brett sat in the dugout at Royals Stadium, enjoying the shade. He was groomed for batting practice, sporting his usual half day's growth of stubble and a yellow T-shirt. He held a fresh chew of tobacco in his right hand and began to wrap bubble gum around it in thin, longitudinal lines. "I get frustrated sometimes and kick my helmet," Brett said, trying to explain a point about Hal McRae. "Well, last night, in Chicago, I tried to kick it and *missed*." Brett shook his head woefully. "Anyway, a guy was getting on me from right above our dugout and about the eighth inning of the game I threw my chew at him. And Mac said, 'The fans got to you, didn't they?'"

"I said, 'No, they didn't. It's just that the guy kept calling me a cocksucking faggot and I don't like to be called that.'"

Brett shrugged. "Mac said, 'You can't let 'em get to you. You've gotta smile 'em off.'"

Brett examined his handiwork and adjusted the gum meridians with his thumbs. "I kinda thought about it and said, 'Well, maybe I was wrong throwing my chew at him, because the next inning [Royals pitcher] Marty Pattin almost went into the stands with a bat after some guy."

(The Royals were unpopular guests at Comiskey Park, Brett might have added, partly because McRae had accidentally, but characteristically, enraged the locals after a big game by howling, within earshot of a Chicago sportswriter, "Get me the broom, the big janitorial broom. We're going to sweep these guys!")

Brett shook his head. "Mac is oh-for-sixteen in Chicago. We're in the most crucial series of the year. And the fans are on him. Forty-five thousand people *hate* him. I was batting behind him, so I could hear a lot of the things they were saying. And they were on him heavy. *'We hate you!' 'You black son of a bitch!'*" Brett popped the chew into his mouth and leaned back. "He took it. He just smiled."

Out on the field, in the sunlight, McRae, hatless, was joking with some other players, a couple of bats tucked under his arm. He loved to talk and loved to laugh, but the fans didn't know that. After his one year of temper tantrums and emotional outbursts, McRae had decided that a rigidly controlled temperament suited him better on the field. Whenever he fanned or ran into an out on the base paths, McRae simply walked slowly back to the dugout, his face a mask, as if he were out in his bathrobe to pick up the morning paper. From the grandstand he was, at such times, a cipher. A player without personality. No one on the bench with Brett could remember McRae throwing a helmet, or kicking the dirt in disgust. "He don't do stuff like that now," Brett said. "He doesn't make excuses. I've never heard him say, 'The ump screwed me on that one-and-one pitch and that's why I flew out.' You never hear him say, 'I lost the ball in the sun.' You never hear him say, 'Well, it's not *my* fault.'"

Brett adjusted the bulge of gum and tobacco in his right cheek. "I think the reason people think Mac plays dirty was the way he took out Willie Randolph at second base in the play-offs." Brett referred to McRae's upending of Yankee second baseman Willie Randolph in the sixth inning of game two of the 1977 play-offs, allowing Fred Patek to score from second. The Yankee fans had howled, and a flurry of collisions, fights, and spikings had punctuated the rest of the series. "But you know," Brett continued, "[Catcher] Thurman Munson came into me one time with his spikes high. You know *he* played 'dirty.' He played just as hard as Mac. And I don't think anything's wrong with it." He snorted. "It's a play-off game. You do anything to win a play-off game. You'd throw that ball at your mom's head if she was batting."

"Oh, yeah?" somebody said.

Brett nodded. "If the situation came up and she was a good hitter, you'd drop her."

McRae's laughter came to the dugout from across the field. "Mac doesn't try to hurt anybody," Brett said. "If he was really a dirty player he'd come up with his spikes high instead of his body high."

"Either way, you can get hurt," a writer said.

Brett nodded. *"He*'s gotten hurt a few times. Bruised his ribs breaking up a double play in Chicago. The next time up he swung and just collapsed at home plate and they carried him off the field on a stretcher. That's the type of guy he is. He'll play unless a bone's sticking out of his foot or his side. I've seen him get hit with some good pitches. He just reaches down and rubs some dirt on it and runs to first."

Somebody recalled the time in 1975, when Texas Ranger power pitcher Jim Bibby shattered McRae's helmet with a fastball. "The next day they threw a right-hander, Steve Hargan, I think. And Mac went four-for-four."

"He can play with pain better than anybody," Brett said. "I don't think he's any *stronger* than anybody, I don't think he *runs* any faster than anybody, which he doesn't." Brett snorted. "I think *I* might have even better speed than he does. He just uses every ounce of ability." For example: McRae invariably ran out ground balls. "You watch Texas play. They hit a routine ground ball and they just kinda run straight for the dugout." Brett looked disgusted. "They don't even *go* to first base."

Brett looked thoughtful. "Mac's the one that makes us go. He knows the game as well as anybody, and even if he's hitting .260, like he is right now, people look up to him and say, 'Hey, you're the man, let's get goin'. You're the one that runs this damn team.'"

Outsiders, of course, assumed that *Brett* was the leader of the Royals, but it was not so. For a while, Brett had claimed that he was too young to run the team. He deferred to the veterans like Cookie Rojas, Amos Otis, and Fred Patek. But as age and experience became less a barrier to leadership, he admitted that it was more than that, that he didn't relish the responsibility that McRae had assumed for the Royals. "I just don't think I have the leadership qualities that Mac has," Brett said that afternoon. "When I say something, people laugh. I joke around a lot. I like to go out and have a good time. But when Mac's on the baseball field, he's *serious.*" Brett leaned over again and spit. He looked thoughtful. "You can't have a leader that always fucks around on the field."

George Brett learned to hit in the summer of 1974.

"He was real young and hadn't experienced a lot of success with the bat," McRae remembers. "He wanted to be a long ball hitter, but the way he was trying to accomplish it he couldn't. He held the bat up high like Carl Yastrzemski and he sorta had a long stroke, a loop. It wasn't a compact swing at all." The eager youngster now joined McRae and a few others for the afternoon workouts on the hot synthetic turf. Lau would pitch batting practice wearing his baseball undershirt or a T-shirt, calling out instructions to the hitter from the mound and sometimes walking in to adjust a player's stance. Later, while another coach took the mound, he would watch intently from behind the cage, offering almost inaudible suggestions to the hitter. Sometimes the advice would be monosyllabic: *"more"* or *"closer"* or *"lower."* Other times he would elaborate, expressing his theories of weight transfer, defining the "launching position," stressing the need for "rhythm." Sometimes he would demonstrate a point, stepping into the box and waiting for the ball with his arms and bat seemingly too close to his body to generate a swing, the muscles in his powerful forearms and wrists rippling; the swing coming hard and fast on a downward plane with no sign of a hitch, loop, or a marshaling of resources, as irrevocable as a spring-loaded catapult. The ball rarely skied off his bat; he sprayed hard grounders and line drives in all directions.

"Charley had me move off the plate a little," Brett recalls, "close my stance a little, bend down more. He wanted me to hit the ball from the second baseman around to left field. That was the hardest part, trying to hit the ball the opposite way. I'd never really tried to do it before." Brett's average languished in the lower .200s, but he did not rebel, as McRae had the year before. Charley Lau's warmth and supportiveness—so at variance with his grim visage and taciturn manner—contrasted appealingly with the relentless criticism of Jack Brett. George felt that the then Royals manager Jack McKeon had little to offer as either a teacher or an authority figure, and his loneliness and frustration were transparent to most of his teammates. "You *need* somebody to talk to," Steve Busby says. "You get in a mental rut. Your confidence goes downhill and without someone to talk to you're in bad shape."

"George was a great student," McRae says, remembering how Brett had responded to Lau's patient prodding. "George had the patience and enthusiasm to come out here and work on it every day. I mean *every* day. For months." It would *take* months, Lau told Brett, possibly *years,* before he could entertain hopes of duplicating Hal McRae's "sudden" success of 1974 (McRae finished with a .310 average, 15 homers, and 88 runs batted in). "Charley believed in taking one step at a time," McRae remembers. "He'd start out very slow. If he had a point where he wanted you to be in July he might not tell you, but you'd start in one place and work to this *other* place."

With Brett, Lau *did* set a specific goal: to boost Brett's average to .265 by season's end.

"George seems to resent the implication that he was a natural," sports columnist Mike McKenzie observes. "He wants you to know how hard he worked to be good." One can only guess how much of Lau's program seemed like "work" to Brett, but there was no denying that much of it was drudgery. Hitting a baseball off a tee into a wall was as mind-numbing as calisthenics. But under Lau's patient tutelage his average, like McRae's, began to rise. Brett remembers it as a series of plateaus: they would set a goal of say, .250. If he reached it, they would raise the goal to .265. If he reached .265, they would set it still higher. The one plateau that Lau remembers clearly is .265, which Brett reached with several weeks remaining in the 1974 season. According to Lau, one day Brett came to him and said, "Hey, Lau, I'm not a .265 hitter. I'm not a .280 hitter. I'm a *.300* hitter." For the self-deprecating Brett, it was an astonishing statement, and certainly not one he would make in public. But Lau had him believing in himself. "We had concentrated on hitting everything," Lau remembers: "inside, up, down, curveball, change-up, fastball to the opposite field. And he found out he could do it. He did it one hundred percent of the time. Here was a foundation in his mind, something he could build on."

The lessons did not end in the batting cage. Lau's mechanical advice allowed Brett and McRae to make more consistent contact at the plate, but to really *feast* on pitchers, Lau thought you had to know them inside out. Accordingly, his coaching now took on a mental and psychological emphasis. "He would be coaching first base," Brett remembers, "and he told me every pitch that was coming. And it wasn't picking up something that the pitcher did, it wasn't stealing signs from the catcher—it was knowing how other teams would pitch me. It was knowing the other team's manager, their catcher, their pitcher's best pitch . . . he *knew* that stuff."

"I'm sure a lot of people practiced it," Lau says, "but Ted Williams was the first guy to come out and say, 'Hey, look—pitchers pitch in patterns. *Teams* pitch in patterns. Opposing managers have a *philosophy*. Catchers have a philosophy.'" Lau gave his students that edge. "We'd talk before a game. What does this guy do? How does his ball react? What's the natural spin on his ball?"

"For about a two-year period I'd sit on breaking balls," McRae laughs. "Sitting on a pitch—that ain't guessing. They wore me out on breaking balls my first year, so I was always looking for it after that. The league is in love with the breaking ball anyway. It was a big thrill to hit a low and away slider hard to right field, because not many guys could do it. I'd hit it and laugh all the way to first base. Or sometimes Charley would say, 'Just give up on any ball on the inside of the plate.'" With two strikes, of course, Brett and McRae simply defended the plate. Brett, in particular, became so confident of his ability to put his bat on the ball that he threw dugout tantrums on the rare occasions that he struck out. ("He hates striking out," Jamie Quirk says. "He just *hates* it." Only once has Brett struck out more than forty times in a major league season, and in 1977 he whiffed just twenty-four times in 564 at bats.)

So absorbed was Brett in his pursuit of the .300 mark

that 1974 season that he paid little heed to a gathering storm. After challenging the Oakland A's for most of the season, the Royals disintegrated in September, plummeting in embarrassment to fifth place, thirteen games off the pace. In the season's wreckage, players brooded over the usual nest of grievances and jealousies that lodge in a ball club. And most of their resentment was directed at the manager, Jack McKeon. Some of the complaints about McKeon were valid, others were self-serving, ignoble attempts to make the manager the scapegoat for the Royals collapse. But the inevitable result of the grumbling was to isolate McKeon and to undermine his authority. It was inevitable, some believe, that in that atmosphere McKeon would become jealous of the loyalty and devotion certain Royals lavished on Lau. "It's almost a mystical thing with Charley," explains Royals broadcaster Fred White. "You hear the word 'guru' with him—and it comes pretty close to that."

Was Lau, in fact, *too* close to the players? One sportswriter, remembering the explosive atmosphere in the Royals clubhouse at the end of that season, says, "McKeon's complaint against Lau was the same as Whitey Herzog had later. McKeon would chew out a player or try to discipline a player, and he'd run to Lau, and Lau would always say, 'Aw, fuck him. That son of a bitch, he doesn't know what he's talkin' about.'" Consequently, the manager felt impotent. "And you just can't run an operation like that, whether it's a baseball team, an army, or whatever."

Other observers challenged this characterization of the dispute, right down to the language attributed to

Lau. ("About the strongest thing he ever says," a friend insists, "is 'Heavens' or 'Oh, my.'") Hal McRae will concede that Lau's stature could have undercut an insecure manager's authority, but he says, "If it does, what can I do about it? People believe in Charley and they trust him. It helps if you can have that type of understanding with somebody in authority, like a coach or a manager. It helps a great deal to have that mental strain lifted."

McKeon didn't see it that way, and with three games remaining in the 1974 season, he had Charley Lau demoted to the minors.

Brett was stunned. Depressed. When he got the news, he trudged to the outfield fence in Royals Stadium and threw baseballs against the wall with tears in his eyes. "I was hitting .291 when they fired Charley, but I didn't get a hit the rest of the season," he says, "'cause I was defeated. They took away the man that had made me hit." Brett finished at .282, but he took little satisfaction in the accomplishment. "I think if they'd have kept Charley I'd have come close to hitting .300 that year," he says. "I really believe that."

So devastated were Brett and McRae by Lau's dismissal that they said some intemperate things to the media. Their support for Lau was emotional and sincere, but the impact of their words was to further undermine McKeon's leadership.

In the opening weeks of 1975, the Royals played ball like a club that *wanted* to lose, bitching at every managerial decision and effectively making McKeon's position untenable. Finally, after long speculation, the Royals fired McKeon and hired Whitey Herzog as his replacement. Herzog, in the manner of political revolutionaries who empty the prisons upon seizure of power, quickly rehired Lau as hitting instructor. And sure enough, the exultant Royals immediately resumed hitting and fielding like professionals. "From that day on, it was *great*," Brett recalls. Hitting wasn't difficult with Lau in the dugout. "It was *stealing*." The Royals won ninety-one games, finished second again to the Oakland A's, and again seemed poised on the brink of baseball success. They also could boast of a new .300 hitter—young George Brett, at .308. And, like McRae before him, Brett said he owed it all to Charley Lau.

"I never hit .300 in the minor leagues," Brett likes to remind people, "but I never had Charley Lau in the minor leagues."

The reputation of a teacher is based on the performance and endorsement of his students. The rapid ascendancy of Hal McRae and George Brett into the American League's top ten hitters—coupled with their insistence that their coach had "made" them great hitters—popularized Charley Lau's theories of hitting. For struggling hitters, the road trip to Kansas City became a pilgrimage. Lau could not coach them personally, but they could hang out behind the batting cage with their eyes and ears open. Joe Rudi, left fielder with the World Champion Oakland A's, credited his success to Lau's coaching, saying, "I'd be driving a truck in Modesto today if it weren't for Charley Lau." Yankee outfielder Lou Piniella went beyond testimonials: he made the mechanics of hitting an obsession. A .300 hitter under Lau in Kansas City before being traded to the Yankees in

1974, Piniella continued to hit well in New York but he batted in perpetual anxiety, as if afraid that he would "forget" how to swing. Teammates swore that Piniella spent more time in the batting cage than he did in bed. His habit of practicing his swing, with or without a bat, in restaurants, hotel lobbies, and elevators—all the while babbling hitting theories—was a source of clubhouse humor around the majors. "He'll take twenty-five or thirty swings a game in the outfield," Clint Hurdle laughs. "In the outfield! He's like the kid in Little League who doesn't get any hits and pouts. Lou does it up here, but he's such a nice guy we let him get away with it. In the old ballpark in Kansas City, they say he made the last out of the inning, ran down the first-base line and ran right out of the *stadium*! Just kept running, he was so mad. They say he showed up forty-five minutes later—sweaty, tired, in his uniform but with no cleats."

George Brett had less trouble separating the science of hitting from his life off the field, but his faith in Charley Lau was as strong as anyone's. "Brett told me one time real early in his career," AP sportswriter Doug Tucker recalls, "that he was back home in the winter and he and his dad were messing around with a ball and bat, talking about batting stances, things like that. His dad told him to do it one way and George said, 'Yeah, Dad, but Charley Lau says I should do it *this* way.' And his dad said, 'Fuck Charley Lau.' And George said, 'Well, fuck you, Dad,' and turned around and walked off."

That Jack Brett couldn't compete with Charley Lau as a hitting coach was of little consequence, of course, but he must have felt a few pangs at being displaced in his son's life. "Charley guided George in a lot of things," Brett's mother Ethel says, "and George always respected him more like a father. Charley never got upset with George. If George had a problem he'd go to Charley rather than his dad." Lau, according to Bobby Brett, was an appealing father figure to George because he brought to the role only the "positive stuff"—praise, warmth, loyalty, patience. "You almost have to be with George and Charley to recognize how strong the bond is between them," says Fred White, a close friend of Lau's. "It's kind of hard to define their relationship, really. There's a little father-son, a little brother-brother, a little best friends, a little teacher-pupil. They do things with a *look*." Brett's new manager, Whitey Herzog, could *also* do things with a look, when he was angry—he now took on the hard-guy role on the infrequent occasions when Brett needed discipline, but Brett didn't seem to mind. "We got along great," Brett says of his relationship with Herzog. "All you had to do was go out and play for him." Herzog sometimes coached like Jack Brett had. "He screamed at me a couple of times," Brett smiles. "When I'd make an error that would lose a ball game, he'd mother me all day long. No manager likes his ballplayers when they fuck up." But Herzog was also free with praise for his star third baseman. Herzog's earthy joviality and awesome self-confidence appealed to Brett. "Every day's new," as Brett put it. It was a manager's duty to chew on his players from time to time and the Lau-Herzog combination seemed ideal to the still-maturing Brett. "George obviously has outstanding physical ability," Steve Busby says, "and his makeup is such that given a kick in the butt at the right time and a pat on the back at the right time, he's going to perform amazingly well."

Hal McRae's feelings for Charley Lau were as intense as Brett's and for the same reasons. McRae had come to see himself in a new light following the disastrous 1973 campaign. "I thought about it a lot that winter," McRae says, recalling the kicked helmets and emotional outbursts. "I was mad with everybody, mad at the fans, mad at the manager. Holding grudges and stuff. It makes your day real long." Over the next several years, the McRae personality turned enigmatic. An assassin on the base paths, he was denounced as a dirty player. But who understood this chatty, easygoing, always-smiling Floridian? "Life is too short to go around mad every day," he said—but he played baseball with a vengeance. He defied easy characterization. To the fans, McRae was simply a name in the lineup who lashed doubles down both foul lines and showed up frequently in the newspaper summaries of league leaders. When *Sport* magazine published a feature on McRae, he was apparently the first person to notice that the action picture under the headline was not of him, but of *another* Royal, utility infielder Dave Nelson. "At least he's black," McRae laughed. "They got *that* right."

McRae had learned to laugh off minor slights. The opinions that mattered belonged to his teammates, the manager, and most of all to Charley Lau. McRae's off-the-field life was conventional and family oriented, his horizons defined by television and the backyard fence. "I'm not real adventurous," he mused one day. "A lot of people always feel that they're missin' something.

They're curious about this and that." He smiled and
shrugged. "I don't have any of that." Similarly, at the
ballpark McRae lived mostly within the nurturing triangle defined by himself, George Brett, and Charley
Lau. "We worked together a lot and George and I
respected Charley so much. We'd go out with him, maybe
for dinner or a few beers, and talk for hours. Not just on
the road, either, but here at home." Other Royals, good-
naturedly, began to refer to the three men as "The
Triangle."

"I don't know of three closer people," Lau recalls
fondly. "We were all learning together."

In 1976, Whitey Herzog's first full season as manager,
the Royals Triangle seemed as menacing to American
League pitchers as the notorious Bermuda Triangle,
with one difference—objects that encroached upon the
Royals Triangle usually came out again at high velocity.
For most of the season Brett enjoyed a substantial lead
over McRae in the league batting race. (Brett peaked at
.371 on July 20.) But by September, McRae was in
command, with Brett, the Twins outfielder Lyman
Bostock and perennial batting champion Rod Carew
(enduring an "off" year) battling for second. The Royals,
meanwhile, were displacing the Oakland A's as champions of the West, becoming the first expansion team
ever to win a division crown. To be sure, a September
slump (the word "choke" was not popular in the Royals
clubhouse) produced alarmed headlines studded with
words like "pressure," "futility," "panic," "stumbling,"
and "bumbling." But the Oakland surge fell short. When
the A's lost on the coast on the night of October 2, an

hour or so after the Royals had blown a game to the
Twins in the ninth, 4-3, Kansas City was free to bathe in
the shaky euphoria of its first baseball title. And with
team priorities resolved, Brett and McRae were free to
concentrate on the batting title. Kansas City had never
boasted a batting champion and now it had two contend-
ers. "We had worked together all year to win a pennant,"
McRae remembers. "We were pulling together the whole
season," McRae laughs, "till the last day. Then we were
looking out for ourselves."

The last day. Somewhere in the back of their minds,
the possibility must have lurked—that it might come
down to the last day and that one of them would possibly
leapfrog over the other to win the batting crown. But for
so long McRae had had the lead; and besides, what did it
matter which of Charley's boys won the title? The
important thing was that Rod Carew be thwarted because, as they all recognized, the Minnesota star might
not have another off season for a while. (He didn't, in
fact. Carew hit a sizzling .388 the next year.) Carew
went 3-for-4 against the Royals in the next-to-the-last
game of the season to raise his average to .329, and Brett
and McRae, who had sat out the game, felt his heat. The
averages now were figured to six or seven decimals with
McRae still leading Brett by five thousandths of a point,
.331078 to .331073. It promised to be the closest batting
race since 1970, when California's Alex Johnson and
Boston's Carl Yastrzemski both batted .329, with Johnson winning by decimals.

"It's something Mac wanted real bad," Brett said later,
"and something *I* wanted real bad."

Sunday, October 4, was a sharp clear day with the

shadow of the stadium roof slicing across the field. Nobody had counted out Rod Carew, but photographers put Brett and McRae together for a curious pregame ceremony. "I'd pretend Mac won, and I'd hold up his hand. Then he'd hold my hand up and *I* was number one." There was a ghoulish aspect to such antics. Both players realized that within hours the darkrooms would produce prints with one or the other beaming triumphantly; the mirror images of the loser, unprinted, would remain stillborn on the negatives, documenting an alternative reality: the world of what-ifs.

The final game, of course, had no significance to the 16,665 fans at Royals Stadium other than as a vehicle for deciding the batting champion. Through three and a half innings, the Twins led, 4-0, but Amos Otis' leadoff single in the fourth got the crowd clapping for Brett, who lined a double to right, scoring Otis. Brett was thrown out trying to stretch his hit to a triple, but he trotted back to the dugout with the league lead. McRae promptly singled to regain first place, .33143 to .33126. Meanwhile Carew, retired in his first two appearances, dropped out of the race. But in the seventh, responding to the growing excitement, Carew doubled past Brett into the corner, lifting his average to .3294701. Brett responded in the bottom of the inning with his second double, retaking the league lead from McRae, and as before, McRae immediately singled in his wake, climbing to .3326996. The crowd roared with appreciation and roared again when Carew singled yet again in the ninth, finishing the season at .3305785. But the inning went slow—everyone anticipated the bottom of the ninth when Brett and McRae were scheduled to appear for the last time that season. Had this game been plotted by a Hollywood screenwriter? In another sport they would have called it sudden death. The race boiled down to one turn at the plate for each pretender—Brett first, with McRae waiting impassively in the on-deck circle.

Brett did not have to look to the third-base coach to see if he had the hit sign. But the first two pitches were balls and there was suddenly the worry that a walk might decide the issue. But no—Brett went for the third pitch. It jammed him, actually, and some observers felt the fear of walking had made him swing at a bad pitch. His heart sank the minute he made contact, for it was a high, lazy fly to left field. Please drop! he prayed as he flung away the bat and bolted toward first base, but the long white line he was racing down was just a runway for one last heavy landing. Hal McRae, he knew, was the American League batting champion.

"I still to this day don't know what happened," Brett says, "'cause I didn't see it."

Those who saw it didn't believe it. The left fielder, Steve Brye, playing deep, hurried in for the easy chance, looking up, and just suddenly went vague. The sun was not in his eyes, but he pulled up as if unable to find the ball. Brett didn't know what had happened until a startled roar hit the stadium. The ball had landed in front of Brye, taken a huge hop off the artificial turf, and was now bouncing toward the left-field wall with Brye in hot pursuit. Turning on the afterburners, Brett was churning up dirt between second and third before Brye could corral the baseball, and the crowd roar swelled as Brett rounded third and headed for home. When he slid across home plate, ahead of the throw, the stadium was bedlam. The euphoria in the stands, however, was not felt in the dugout, where confusion quickly turned to dismay: The hit sign was lit on the scoreboard, crediting Brett with an inside-the-park home run. A kind of anguish infected the stunned Royals. Brett seemed bewildered; he again led the American League in hitting, but the lazy ellipse of the cheap hit tormented him.

Hal McRae slapped Brett's hand and grinned as Brett then jogged to the dugout, but an ugly suspicion was clouding McRae's consciousness. A hundred childhood grievances came to mind as he stared out toward left field where Steve Brye stood embarrassed and unmoving, anxious for the season to end. It was McRae's task now to answer Brett's challenge for the third time in a row. He fouled a pitch off, he swung and missed, and now was reduced to defending the plate, the image of Brett's feeble home run still gnawing at his concentration. And then, too quickly, his season was over—a ground ball to shortstop Luis Gomez, a futile sprint down the base path, a throw to first, a dream shattered. The photographers had their champion.

The crowd, of course, did not yet appreciate the events as a calamity. They rose to give McRae a standing ovation as he trotted back to the dugout, and he responded at first, by doffing his helmet. But suddenly, like the rupturing of a blood vessel, McRae's stoicism failed him, ugly suspicions flooded his mind. He turned toward the Twins dugout and—there was no mistaking it—made a vulgar gesture with his arm and fist in the direction of Twins manager Gene Mauch. Before the gesture had fully registered on the shocked crowd— there was a mass gasp, a collective "What the?"—Gene

Mauch and McRae were charging each other across the infield. Umpires and a few players intercepted and restrained the two angry men before they could get at each other, but the benches and bullpens emptied of players in the obligatory ritual. No one wanted to fight on the last day of the season, and the swarm of baffled players milling together on the field made a fitting chorus for this most strangely concluded batting race.

"This is America," a subdued but emotional McRae told reporters in the clubhouse afterward. "Not much has changed." The words came out slowly as McRae fought back tears. He believed, the reporters gathered, that Mauch had ordered Steve Brye to play Brett deeper than usual in the ninth inning, so that Brett—a white man—would win the batting title. "I know they let the ball drop," he said; "that I lost it isn't the big thing, the way I lost is."

There was no champagne and celebration in the Royals clubhouse. Sensitive to McRae's disappointment, his teammates and media people shuffled around, talked in hushed voices, quietly debated the roles of Mauch and Brye in the climactic ninth. The Royals seemed confused as to what the Twins' motivation might be in conspiring against McRae—race was mentioned by a few, resentment toward McRae for his aggressive base running by others, but most preferred not to speculate. Cookie Rojas, who had played for Mauch at Philadelphia, didn't believe that the Twins manager would plot against McRae, but in the confusion of the moment he wasn't above suspecting Brye. "I told our players," Rojas told reporters, "that I pray to God that the sun which gives us light every day was in Steve Brye's eyes. If not, I hope his conscience bothers him every day of his life." The *Kansas City Star*'s Joe McGuff, who doubted that Mauch had plotted the misplay, reported from the Twins clubhouse that Mauch had seemed genuinely shaken, bowing his head over his desk and moaning, "Oh, God! You play so hard all year long and then end up on a note like this. It's sickening." It was unlikely that Mauch, of all people, bore a grudge against McRae for his aggressiveness as a player—McRae was the prototype of the combative player Mauch admired. As McGuff wrote later, "Mauch might incite a riot or might be guilty of using the worst language this side of [baseball executive] Frank Lane— but no matter how much he might dislike a player, I don't think he would ever attempt to cheat him out of a batting title."

As for Brye, he took full responsibility for his position-ing on the Brett homer. "I messed up," he said. "I made the mistake of playing too deep on my own." Brye had little else to say except, "I didn't see it too good," so the one man on the field who knew for certain if his misplay was "motivated" receded into the background of the controversy. "I trust Steve Brye implicitly," Gene Mauch said, "and if I didn't, I'd run him out of baseball."

Back in the Royals clubhouse, McRae's explosion had had a sobering effect on his white friends. They saw for the first time the profound well of hurt and anger that resided inside this most genial and uncomplaining of black men. "I cried," Charley Lau admits. "I was happy for George and sad for Mac, but it wasn't a fair thing. I wouldn't like to go through that again." There was a burst of speculation: could the commissioner of baseball declare the batting race a tie? "George wanted to make it half and half," Lau recalls, "or to cut the championship bat in two. Cookie Rojas and I thought we'd get 'em *two* bats, if we had to buy one ourselves."

Brett—whom one writer called "the most unhappy of champions"—looked as though he wanted to hide. "I felt funny afterwards," he recalls, "because everybody was consoling Mac, saying, 'Hey! he got screwed.' And here I had won the batting title and no one says shit to me. Mr. [Ewing] Kauffman [owner of the Royals] comes into the locker room, he's got his arms around Mac, and Mac's got his head in his locker, and I'm there three or four stalls away, sittin' by myself. And I'm saying to myself, I just won the batting title and no one's around."

The frustrating part for Brett was his helplessness, the knowledge that nothing he said or did could alter the reality of his lame home run. "I hated to see Mac hurt like that. You had two teammates who were the best of friends, and it comes down to the last inning of the last game of the year, something that I don't think either of us had ever dreamed about. We'd always batted right next to each other, we'd had good years together. It took a lot of the fun out of it."

In fact, it took all of the fun out of it. According to Lau, "George's statement was, 'Give it to Mac. I'm gonna win one sooner or later anyway.'" But there was no way to "give" McRae the title. An investigation of the incident revealed nothing. Lee MacPhail, the president of the American League, announced several days later that he was satisfied that Brett was the legitimate champion. "This office has questioned many people with respect to the last day of the batting race in the American League," McPhail declared. "Although it is not always possible to know with certainty what governs men's actions, there is no evidence or reason to believe that any players in the game of October 4, at Kansas City, were unfairly motivated. Lacking such, it is unjust to imply otherwise simply by citing one misplay. A season of baseball includes many great plays and inevitable misplays."

"Life's not always fair," McRae laughed later, when he had overcome his disappointment. "George felt bad about it, but what could he do?" As unfair as that last hit had seemed, McRae agreed that it was equally unfair that Brett should feel apologetic and let down after his championship season. "It was really *my* fault that I lost," McRae said, "'cause I was leading by a big margin the first part of September. I shoulda won by fifteen or twenty points, but I hit a slump."

Brett would pile up award after award in the years to come, but McRae's career would become ironically obscured, cast in shadow by the man who had learned so much from him. "I've completely recovered from the incident." McRae insists. But to a ballplayer, a batting title (like a Cy Young Award or an MVP trophy) ensures one of baseball immortality. One gets invited to more banquets. One is referred to as "the former American League batting champion" instead of "former major leaguer." One's obituary is longer.

George Brett won the American League batting crown in 1976.

"He hit .333," McRae explains. "I hit .332."

McRae slipped in 1978. After batting .298, with 21 homers and 92 RBIs in 1977, he struggled through most of the summer at a below .260 pace. Word leaked out after a while that he had a sore shoulder, and if pursued on the subject, McRae allowed that the soreness was annoying. "I broke my shoulder playing tennis," he laughed, "on my backhand. It popped." When asked to explain his troubles at the plate, though, he usually talked mechanics. "My problems stem from trying to hit home runs early in the year," he said. "I really don't have any excuses because I didn't have to try that. Nobody made me do it." He shrugged. "But still, I've had time to adjust and I just can't get back to doing the things I used to do. Pullin' is just"—he smiled and hesitated—"when you're not a pull hitter, pullin' just destroys a hitter." He laughed. "Hopefully, I'm not destroyed."

Manager Herzog did not buy the argument that a home run appetite had given McRae the cramps. "Bullshit," he said. "Mac's big enough to hit home runs—he hit twenty-one last year. Since he *stopped* hitting home runs his average has dropped." Herzog snorted. "Hit it hard, don't worry about where it goes." He thought instead that McRae's sore shoulder might be affecting his swing. The joint appeared swollen most of the time, and it didn't seem to heal. Herzog restricted McRae's already rare outfield appearances even further, confining him to his regimen of "Tunnel Olympics" interrupted by a few turns at the plate. One night, when he did pencil the surprised McRae in at left field, Herzog pointed vaguely at the outfield and said, "Don't worry, Mac, we'll take you out there and show you where it's at."

McRae was more interested in rediscovering, "where it's at" at the plate. He seemed suddenly incapable of hitting the ball hard to right field, which interested onlookers attributed to his stance, his grip, his eyesight, his age, his color, or his attitude. One sympathetic observer—the late Dick Mackey, sports columnist for the *Kansas City Times*—thought that Charley Lau had messed up McRae's stance. "There's no way McRae can hit a baseball with his arms and legs like that," the always desolate-looking Mackey muttered from the press box, sighing deeply at every pop-up, feeble grounder, and called third strike. Shortly before his untimely death that season, Mackey even approached golfer Tom Watson at an awards luncheon to get a golfer's analysis of McRae's weight transfer and the clearing of his hips. Mackey, it was apparent, accepted McRae's public explanation: that his slump was caused by temporary flaws in his swing. Unwittingly, of course, McRae's refusal to alibi tarnished the image of Charley Lau as a "slump ender."

Many major leaguers look *up* to a .260 average, but McRae was discouraged. "I really feel I should hit. 320 or .330, if I don't hit a lot of home runs," he said. "If I hit a lot of home runs, I should *still* hit .300." He shook his head. "Lately, to keep from thinking about what's going on, I just sleep all day. Sleep as much as I can."

The fans began to get impatient. There was no place in baseball, they grumbled, for a designated hitter who couldn't hit. Even McRae's defenders, those who called Don Burley's KMBZ *Telesports* show to scold the vultures who constantly circled the Royals, thought that McRae should be benched long enough for his sore shoulder to heal. Kansas Citians, when asked, tended to grossly underestimate McRae's good years with the

Royals, tricked by the paucity of recollectable images. Even those who were close to McRae and admired him shared the view that he was, somehow, a diminished star, underappreciated and plagued by bad fortune. "He was one of the best-looking second basemen I'd ever seen in the minor leagues," recalled Royals coach Steve Boros, a former Detroit Tiger infielder who played with McRae at Buffalo in 1967. An accident in winter ball, he recalled, had destroyed McRae's promise as an infielder. Sliding into home plate in a Puerto Rican League game, McRae had fractured his leg in four places. Two operations—to insert, and later remove, a rod from his leg—had stolen McRae's agility and left him with a different walk. "He just wasn't the same player after he broke that leg," Boros said. "I thought when I first saw him again at Fort Myers, years after the injury, that he walked with a limp." Boros nodded toward McRae, walking across the field with short jerky steps, his legs looking graceless under a prominent rear end. "I think there are times *now* that you see it."

The unspoken thought in the clubhouse was that McRae had lost it. "If he'd a been a horse, we'd a shot him," a teammate joked later. McRae even began doubting himself, and when reporters tactfully began asking him his plans after baseball, he answered that he hoped to operate a clothing store back home in Bradenton, Florida, specializing in women's and babies' fashions. "I want something small," he said, "not the hustle-bustle-type business. I'd like to just make enough so I can leave the problems at the shop in the afternoon." The terror of the base paths added, "I don't wanna have to hustle."

Still, McRae made no excuses for his play. Showed no

anger. Threw no tantrums. "Nobody wants to sit around and hear you complain," he said. "It's kind of boring to listen to a ballplayer complain." His teammates were awed by his composure. "Coping with frustration? He's the best I've ever seen," John Wathan said. "He doesn't get excited whether he has a good game or a bad game." U. L. Washington, mired on the bench behind veteran Fred Patek, thought *he* had troubles. "Sometimes I would have bad attitudes," Washington recalls. "I would ignore a lot of people. But I would talk to McRae and he'd say, 'Hey, they don't care about you being mad. When you're goin' bad, the only thing that you can do is go a little harder.'"

McRae obviously enjoyed his reputation as a dignified elder statesman of baseball. "I think the younger, better players are usually a lot more emotional," he said, "because they don't have to think that much. They have enough natural ability to get mad and throw something and go out and get a base hit. But I'm a bit older and I don't have the same ability those guys have. Throwing stuff won't make any difference to me. When I get mad now, I sit down. My ears may be burning, but I won't show any emotion. I *think* a lot more than I used to. I try to think it out rather than have an outburst."

Something, too, had turned Hal McRae into a supreme realist. Mike McKenzie put it succinctly one day over a steak at Kansas City's Hereford House. "Hal McRae, to me, is a many-faceted individual that revolves around this axis," McKenzie said, balancing a steak knife on one finger, "that spells *money*." One time in spring training, McKenzie had heard McRae dispense one of his favorite sayings: "As long as the eagle flies on Friday!" McKenzie laughed. "I said, 'Hal, that's the most telltale remark you've ever made. 'Cause that's where you end and begin.'"

McRae would not have denied it. "I wouldn't say I'm a mercenary," he joked, "but I'm a ballplayer for hire." Once, when asked how he maintained such an unruffled positive attitude, McRae replied that playing baseball had realized his childhood dreams. "Poor kids," he said, "dream more than people that got stuff." McRae's mother, when she wasn't ill, had worked as a maid and his father was a gardener. There were eleven children. "We didn't have a lot," he recalls, "but we had as much as other people around us, so it wasn't something that you were real conscious about. The house was warm and we had enough to eat." Still, there were reminders that dreams cost more if you lived on the wrong side of town. There was no Little League for blacks in Avon Park, Florida, so McRae learned to play on the sandlots. Later he noticed that the white high schools played at night, before big crowds, and got covered by the newspaper. "That sorta of bothered me, but it was something I learned to live with." Segregation? "I was aware of it. You were sorta unconcerned, as long as people didn't bother you."

As long as the eagle flies on Friday. "That's the neighborhood expression," McRae laughs. "I grew with it. Being a guy from a poor background, money is important to me. The best thing I can do is give my kids a good education, and it takes money to do that." Once, when asked if he feared that he'd quickly be forgotten at the end of his playing career, McRae replied, "The only fear that I have about retirement is that I don't wanna be broke. I don't wanna be talked about as a guy that played thirteen, fourteen, fifteen years, and look at him now, he ain't got nothin'. He threw all his money away. *That's* my fear.

"The rest of it? If I'm forgotten, that's fine. But if I can hold my head up and stand tall after I get out, and be a respected citizen in the community—and if people feel, 'He's not a dummy' . . . then I'll be happy."

McRae's pragmatism, in 1978, kept him from bailing out too soon. "I'm gonna take all I can get," he joked. "The way they're paying now—as long as they'll pay, I'll play!" He broke out of his slump one night in July against the California Angels, cracking a two-run triple and stroking his one thousandth hit, an eighth-inning home run that curled around the left-field foul pole. The standing ovation he received as he trotted back to the dugout may have relieved some of his anxieties—he wore that pleasant boyish smile—but after the game he did not celebrate by squirting fire extinguishers or kicking down doors. He went home, instead, watched the *Untouchables* on TV, and then went to sleep.

McRae, it was learned after the season's end, had played all year with a torn rotator cuff. The same injury had wrecked the careers of the Royals star pitcher, Steve Busby, and Milwaukee Brewers slugger Larry Hisle, among others, and was reportedly so painful and debilitating that simply combing one's hair was an ordeal. Suddenly, the mysteries of McRae's strange stances and of Lau's apparently ineffective coaching were dispelled. "Mac couldn't put his arm over his head," Royals second baseman Frank White recalls, "so he couldn't hit the high pitch." Busby—for whom the sleepless nights and nagging pain were a still-fresh memory—now understood why McRae could not drive the ball to right center field, his specialty. "What he did instead was try to compensate by the way he attacked a pitcher," Busby said. For years, Hal McRae had been notorious for always taking the first pitch, merely glancing at it as it hissed by, as if to ascertain that the pitcher was indeed throwing baseballs and not onions or cantalopes. In 1978, McRae had begun swinging at first pitches. Now everyone knew why. He had been trying to capitalize on the book on him. McRae's final statistics for 1978, previously described as "disappointing," suddenly attained heroic stature. McRae had recorded 641 at bats with his maimed shoulder, had hit 16 home runs, had driven in 72, had batted .273, and had stolen 17 bases— all with a torn rotator cuff. "It bothered me in every phase of life," he admitted later, and he agreed that he should have had surgery that spring. "But I didn't know what I had," he protested. "I thought it would go away."

The diagnosis of McRae's injury seemed to put the cap on his career. None of the Royals would say out loud that their aggressive DH was through, but when he returned from surgery that spring with a wicked scimitar of scar tissue across his shoulder, he was greeted with a little more deference by his teammates. George Brett, in particular, worried about the team's direction without a healthy Hal McRae. The insights that Brett acknowledged came to him from McRae were often the stuff capsulized as "baseball wisdom"—the seldom-followed verities such as, "Run out ground balls and pop-ups," "Learn to read the outfielders," and "Slide hard into second." But the most important lesson that McRae taught him was this: that to achieve success as a ballplayer, frustration had to be coped with. "You've got to do what's right for you," Brett said, marveling at McRae's self-control. "You watch other guys, like Lou Piniella, who goes bananas, who goes *crazy* every time he makes an out." Brett shrugged. "Lou's had some great years. And Pete Rose! Every time you see Pete Rose he's in a big argument with somebody, he's goin' crazy." Brett painted a vivid word portrait of the inimitable Rose disputing an umpire's call—arms waving and jaw working furiously, those incongruous little boy's bangs bouncing with every stomp of his feet. "I don't think I take the game quite as seriously as Pete does," Brett laughed.

Yes and no. Brett's code of self-control was not as stifling as McRae's. After being decked by a Milt Wilcox fastball in 1980, a furious Brett waited until *after* he had batted to confront the Tiger pitcher, but he still precipitated a bench-clearing brawl that got him ejected. ("I didn't want to miss my turn at bat over it," Brett explained afterward.) Mostly, Brett dealt with frustration in the time-honored, destructive, cathartic style favored by Rose and Piniella. His concession to McRae and maturity was to throw most of his tantrums in private—usually in the dark recesses of the tunnel—after a particularly feeble plate appearance or after a fielding miscue. "When I'm gonna explode, the guys know it," Brett says. "If they're in the runway, they just leave. And I'll just destroy a helmet or beat the hell out of a trash can. I just have to exert so much energy in beating up a trash can or throwing my helmet up against the wall."

Brett's outbursts were once as common as summer

thunderstorms and about as loud. "I think he led the league in destroying helmets," John Wathan recalls. "They ordered them by the dozens for him." Sometimes the results were comical. One time a couple of Royals ventured timidly into the tunnel when the rampaging Brett had quieted down and found their star third baseman sitting inside a large trash can, peering over the top edge with a silly grin on his face. Sometimes the Royals didn't know whether to laugh or fret. According to Charley Lau, "George used to beat the walls and the wastebaskets to the point where we were scared he was going to hurt himself." Brett recalls one such rage of extraordinary proportions: "I almost got hurt once doing it," he laughs. "I slipped on the asphalt floor and landed on my back . . . so I got madder and threw a shopping cart and fell down again. It takes everything out of you, you get tighter and tighter until you just lay on the ground with a sigh of relief."

Anyone familiar with psychological trends knew that Brett's tantrums were more in fashion in mental health circles than McRae's repression of anger and frustration. His childish rages were a figurative upchucking of tensions; as Brett described it, "Afterwards you can relax and go out on the field feeling a lot better." Similarly, many baseball people contended that Brett possessed a perfect baseball temperament. Childish, yes—but that was his strength. ("He *plays* baseball," Jamie Quirk says. "That's what makes George as good as he is.") But Brett could never have been a great ball-player if he hadn't emulated Hal McRae's rockbed approach to frustration: which was that one dared not succumb to self-pity. The child in Brett—in anybody—

wants to quit when the game stops being fun. "When you're not having a good year," Brett admits, "it's hard to give it everything you've got. You're depressed, you're down on yourself." That happened in the spring of 1979, when Brett tried to play while recovering from off-season surgery on his right thumb. "The first month of the season I didn't give one hundred percent everyday," he confessed later, "'cause I was really having a shitty year. On May tenth, I think, I had only one home run, seven RBIs, and was hitting about .240." Like McRae, Brett was willing to play with pain, but he didn't pretend that he was above it. Why, then, had he insisted on playing hurt? "Because I think I help the ball club win." He quickly added: "I'm not the *reason* we win, but I'm one of the reasons. The thumb was sound, a lot of it was in my head."

Also in Brett's head was the very fresh memory of Hal McRae playing with a torn rotator cuff, playing all out, playing without excuses or alibis. "We played that year before two and a third million people in Kansas City," Brett remembers. "Out of six years, I'd had five good years. I'd hit .300 four times, and when you've done that, more people are watching you. I thought, if I dog it, people will look at me and say, 'He's the biggest dog I've ever seen!'" Self-pity, he decided, would produce nothing but further embarrassment. "In the last five months I busted my ass like no one ever has."

That was the year that George Brett left Hal McRae back in the shadows. In 1979, despite his slow start, Brett hit .329, scored 119 runs, drove in 107 runs, and led the league in hits with 212 and triples with 20. But teammates saw much in Brett's performance that reminded them of Hal McRae in his prime—the daring, the doggedness, the hustle. They even saw flashes of Mac in Brett's temperament. The outbursts seemed more ritualistic now, the emotional slumps less profound. "He's not nearly as volatile as he used to be," John Wathan said, "and a lot of that has to do with Hal, watching him day in and day out, seeing the way he handles it." It was still difficult not to link the two ballplayers.

One play stood out, the sort of vivid exercise of baserunning genius that lodges forever in a fan's memory. One night in Royals Stadium, in a game with the Red Sox, Brett was on second base when a teammate launched a drive to deep left center field. The ball did not look catchable and Brett ran almost to third base without having tagged up at second—only to turn and see center fielder Fred Lynn making a back-to-the-plate catch on the warning track. Brett had to race back to second to prevent the double play. But Lynn, playing it safe, took a little off his throw to the infield. Brett, sliding into second at full speed, scrambled up instantly and raced back toward third while the baffled cutoff man turned, clutching the ball, and tried to figure out where Brett had gone. His throw bounced a few feet behind the sliding Brett at third. Brett calmly slapped the dust off his pants while the crowd roared, delighted to lay claim to such a mischievous scalawag—but fulfilled more deeply as well, for it was a play that only a great player, a player of supreme confidence, would have dared to attempt. It was a Hal McRae play. A study in opportunism.

But one knew, somehow, that McRae, the teacher, would not have been safe. His instincts were not sharp

George Brett, age eleven
(Jack Brett)

Ken Brett, age eleven
(Jack Brett)

Photos are by Hank Young unless otherwise indicated.

Opposite: Ken Brett. A posed shot taken at El Segundo's Recreation Park. "My life was very simple. I went to school, played ball, came home, did my homework, went to bed. I didn't even have a girlfriend." *(Jack Brett)*

Below: Bobby Brett scores for his college team. "George doesn't do a thing unless he talks to Bobby," their mother says. "He's the organizer. Bobby says, 'We're gonna do it *this* way,' and that's the way we do it." *(Jack Brett)*

Overleaf: George Brett, shortstop, El Segundo High School. "He was a *great* player. He *wasn't* mediocre." —Coach John Stevenson *(Jack Brett)*

"George is not exactly a flake, but he's not exactly your basic, brooding genius, either." —Jim Murray, Los Angeles *Times*

George contemplates a knock-down pitch.

"His concentration is just incredible." —Jamie Quirk

George makes a soft throw in a rundown at Royals Stadium.

George Brett and Ken Brett—teammates on the Royals

John Mayberry—"Big John"—the slick-fielding slugger whose troubles at the plate exacerbated the coaching differences between Whitey Herzog and Charley Lau.

Whitey Herzog. "He wants *power!*" Clint Hurdle laughs. "That's why Whitey left Kansas City. He got too big for the organization. Now he's at St. Louis, pulling all the strings."

Ewing Kauffman—the pharmaceutical millionaire and Royals owner

Morganna—"Baseball's Kissing Bandit"

Hal McRae. "When he talks, I listen," says Brett. "He's the leader. He's the one that makes us go."

Charley Lau (foreground) and Whitey Herzog: "the Svengali of Swat" and "the White Rat"

"There's nothing that George does with a bat that surprises me. If George's goal was .400 and winning had nothing to do with it—I think he could."—Charley Lau

George demonstrates his "pre-Hal McRae Rule" slide into—or rather *over*—second base on a double-play ball, upsetting the Brewer shortstop. The ensuing discussion turns ugly.

"I was never a good fielder in the minor leagues. I made a few errors and got a little defensive out there. But I've gained a lot of confidence."

Introductions at Royals Stadium before the second game of the 1980 American League Championship Series. Two nights later, outfielder Willie Wilson (blowing bubble) would double with two out in the sixth, shortstop U. L. Washington would beat out an infield hit, and George would clear the bases by launching a Goose Gossage fastball into the upper deck in Yankee Stadium for the Royals' first pennant.

George at the New Stanley Bar in Westport in 1977. "I didn't get tired of Westport," he says. "I think they got tired of me."

George poses with the famous empty fridge at Animal House, Fairway, Kansas, 1977.

Above: Left to right, Jamie Quirk, George Brett, John Wathan (hidden), Marty Pattin and Ken Brett.

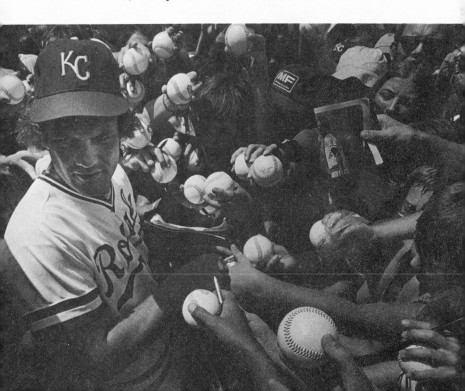

enough, his legs were not fast enough, and he was simply not as *lucky,* if you believe in luck, as George Brett, the pupil.

"I guess everybody wants to be liked," Hal McRae had said in response to the question about his "dirty" play, "but I wouldn't compromise to be liked." There was a certain belligerence to the words, but a quiet earnestness to his voice and a child's vulnerability in his eyes.

In the end, for Hal McRae, it would not be a question of being liked . . . but of being remembered.

2. Coach in Exile

Baseball is no longer a pastoral game, but the notion that baseball fans are more patient than other sports fans—so many farmers sitting on fence rails, chewing straw and watching semipro teams play under a sun crawling lazily across the sky—is still appealing and widely held. It was, perhaps, even true up to 1920. That was the year that Babe Ruth was given the keys to Yankee Stadium and pitchers were given a new, juiced-up baseball to throw to him. The resulting fifty-four home runs produced an amphetaminelike restlessness in baseball fans, who regarded the new star, the Bambino, as an exciting and unstable force capable of producing runs in bunches, with quick, fearsome swings of the bat. They became disenchanted with bunters and singles hitters, with dirty-suited sociopaths who spiked opponents, ducked beanballs, and stole bases. There was something majestic about a blow struck so soundly that the ball actually left the arena of play. That's why they called Ruth "the Sultan of Swat." The home run was inexorable. Lordly.

In 1976, as Charley Lau's reputation swelled on the achievements of George Brett and Hal McRae, quick-witted writers began calling the previously anonymous coach "the Svengali of Swat." The Svengali tag suited the extraordinary trust and loyalty he inspired in his students; but it had an ignoble ring to it as well, implying that Lau got his results through trickery, machinations, or illusions. If home runs were regal, then singles and doubles, in the eyes of some fans, were inevitably lesser hits. McRae hit fifteen home runs with his .310 average in 1974, but the following year he hit only five, and in 1976, challenging for the batting title, just eight. Brett showed even less power, producing only two, eleven, and seven homers over the same years. Those low figures, combined with the fact that neither star had ever driven in a hundred runs over a season, encouraged the criticism that Lau's boys were hitting for "empty" average. The Royals were often dismissed as "Punch and Judys" for their combination of line-drive hitting and speed on the base paths—a sobriquet which particularly annoyed Lau, who believed that spacious Royals Stadium was a graveyard for free swingers. He also considered it a willful misrepresentation of his theories to say he didn't "like" or "believe" in hitting home runs. "I get as excited as anyone else when one of our guys knocks one out of the park," he later wrote in *The Art of Hitting .300,* "particularly if it comes at a crucial moment in a game." *Trying* for home runs, however, was an advanced technique that Lau believed young hitters should forgo, learning, instead, to make consistent contact with sound fundamentals. The novelty of this approach, in the majors, partly explained Lau's reluctance to walk out on the field and take command. ("Charley's a very approachable guy," a close friend says, "but *you* have to approach him. He knows you have to believe totally in him or you're not gonna get anywhere with what he teaches.") Lau became accustomed to bewildered stares when he told rookies he didn't expect—or necessarily *want*—them to hit home runs. "You're drilled from the age of eight or nine years old to swing with power," John Wathan recalls. "They say, 'You're a big guy, you gotta hit home runs!'" Lau told them just the opposite, and it was unsettling. "Charley helped me more than anybody else has." Wathan says. "He changed my swing around completely—but sometimes it's tough to adjust to a new way of thinking at the age of twenty-two or twenty-three." To some youngsters, the shattering of the dream of hitting dozens of homers in the majors was analogous to a black kid's stunned awakening to the fact that he won't grow up to be president. To these players, Charley Lau was not Svengali. He was Scrooge.

There was a lingering suspicion among fans addicted to Big Bang baseball that Lau was actually suppressing home runs, diffusing the power potential of his stars. Close attention was paid, therefore, to the career of John Mayberry, the Royals lone undisputed power hitter. Mayberry was a muscular, slick-fielding first baseman who had appeared in only 105 games in four years with the Houston Astros. But in 1972, his very first season as a Royal, Mayberry belted 25 home runs while hitting an eye-opening .298 and driving in 100 runs. The following year, he hit 26 home runs and drove in *another* 100. He seemed to be a left-handed version of Milwaukee Brewers slugger George "Boomer" Scott, and a strong argument against the "powerless" tag put on the Royals. In 1974, an off year hampered by injury, Mayberry fell off to twenty-two home runs, and for half of 1975 he waved at baseballs as if they were darting manifestations of a disco mirror ball. But then, one July night in Arlington, Texas, he broke out of his slump, launching three home runs into the darkness beyond the right-field wall. He had only hit nine home runs before that night in Texas, but for the rest of the summer John Mayberry did an impersonation of Babe Ruth in his prime, finishing with thirty-four home runs and a .291 average. Even spacious Royals Stadium could not contain his towering blasts, which splashed into the right-field water spectacular, dented the bullpen car, and bounced high off the concrete steps into the concession stand far behind the right-field general admission seats. Many other blasts parachuted to outfielders on the warning track in center field, or ricocheted high off the walls, as Mayberry lumbered into second base. (He had thirty-eight doubles that year—one triple.) Pitchers walked him a league-leading 119 times, usually drawing a chorus of boos from Royals fans enthralled by the thunder in Mayberry's bat. They dubbed him "Big John," and no one had to ask why.

"John wasn't a pull hitter in the beginning," McRae remembers. "He was an alley-type hitter. But when he started hitting the home runs, he started pulling more." Opposing teams began to play their shortstop to the right of second base, moved the second baseman into short right field, put two outfielders on the warning track, and offered Mayberry several acres of left field to shoot at. Mayberry, ignoring the invitation, pinwheeled his bat menacingly behind his head and lashed pitch after pitch to right field. Nobody kept count of the times Big John was thrown out by second basemen who speared his rocketing grounders and short-hopped his liners in shallow right field, bouncing throws to first before Mayberry could cross the bag. Except, maybe, Charley Lau. Mayberry's "taters"—those extraterrestrial shots that soared into the blackness above the right-field foul pole and bombed into the dollar-fifty seats an eternity later—made believers of everybody else.

Naturally, when John Mayberry stopped hitting, the fans turned vicious. He slumped to 13 home runs and a .232 average in 1976, the Royals first championship season. Kansas City is a notoriously polite baseball town, but the sight of a big, powerful guy striking out or popping-up drew the ire and ridicule of impatient fans. Even Mayberry's still-robust 95 RBIs didn't satisfy his detractors, who complained that they came mostly on sacrifice flies or grounders, and were therefore, inexplicably, undeserved. "He ought to listen to Charley Lau and hit to left field," some fans argued, suddenly convinced that Mayberry was a stupid hitter. His next season—a 23 homer season with a lowly .230 average and 13 fewer RBIs—produced more divergent viewpoints. Some believed, now, that it was *Lau*'s fault that Mayberry had faltered, that he had been robbed of his power and his confidence by the "Svengali of Swat."

Whitey Herzog's impatience with the frustrated slugger was widely reported, and fans were divided over whether Mayberry's failings were the consequence of too little coaching or too much coaching. Mayberry was still an asset to the Royals on *defense,* all agreed—particularly for his skill in snaring errant throws—but there is always something pathetic about a frustrated slugger, a sense of impotence and futility that alarms the fans and make some howl for his banishment. (Expressed, of course, in vocal shorthand as *"Boooo!"*)

Lau's position, all along, had been that Mayberry's pull-hitting strategy, although devastating in the short run, made him vulnerable to long slumps. The pull hitter, he argued, had to get his bat on the ball well out in front of the plate—requiring a fast bat, an early commitment to swing, and a knack for "guessing" pitches correctly. Anything short of a perfect combination of the three, Lau said, led to an out. Lau's philosophy was not necessarily endorsed by Whitey Herzog, who *wanted* his strong hitters to aim for the fences, but manager and coach agreed that Mayberry had become a reluctant student, deaf to their suggestions. "John Mayberry was one of those guys who didn't want to take the time and do the work," Brett said later. But everyone agreed that Mayberry's case was exceptional—a player for whom hitting had been, perhaps, too easy. Herzog had seen, with his own eyes, John Mayberry smacking baseballs as though they were sitting on a tee. But as the memory of those feats dimmed and as Mayberry doggedly refused to change his philosophy of hitting, Herzog became more and more disenchanted with his big first baseman. When Mayberry struck out twice, bobbled a double-play attempt, and dropped a critical pop-up in the fourth game of the 1977 championship series (and later offered that he had taken a pain pill for a tooth infection and was ill), Herzog benched him and reportedly delivered general manager Joe Burke an ultimatum: to trade Mayberry in the off-season. With rumors about Mayberry and his attitude rife in baseball, Burke was able to do little more the following spring than dump Mayberry on the Toronto Blue Jays in return for a small cash payment.

For the Royals, who took a horse trader's pride in getting the better of their infrequent deals, the Mayberry "trade" was the most one-sided and inept transaction in club history. The Royals platooned various players at first base the next two years, but none who could match Mayberry either as power hitter or glove man. (Herzog even considered moving either Brett or Amos Otis into the void, to the delight of the former and the chagrin of the latter.) The fans, conveniently forgetting the booing of Mayberry, now cheered Big John when he visited Royals Stadium wearing Blue Jays blue, and lambasted Burke for "giving away" the Royals talent. Mayberry was generally diplomatic and forgiving on his visits to Kansas City, but he couldn't resist a little sniping from Toronto. "We've got a batting instructor here who doesn't believe in messing with your stance," he said. "He gets you thinking you can hit anything they throw." Nonetheless, Mayberry, over the next few seasons, continued to combine twenty-plus home runs with medium average hitting, with one difference only: in Toronto, he was the most stellar of the last place Jays.

*   *   *

In some ways, John Mayberry's decline seemed to strengthen Charley Lau's position on the Royals. If so great a talent as Mayberry could not consistently hit the ball trying to pull with power, then what chance had the less powerful Royals? Most were inclined to follow the Lau program. "I found it real hard to stay in the stance he put me in," Frank White remembers, "but he helped me out quite a bit with situations, pitch locations, that sort of thing. His biggest asset to me was to get me to relax, to get the tension out of my wrists and forearms." Another young Lau protégé, bespectacled right fielder Al Cowens, experimented with an outlandish-looking stance in which the bat "drooped"—hung limply from his hands, barrel downward. Cowens leaped from 3 to 23 homers, drove in 112 runs, hit .312, and finished third for American League MVP.

Gradually, though, a Charley Lau backlash became discernible in the wake of the Mayberry debacle. Whereas before it had been the mark of the insider to know about the unheralded coach and to attribute the Royals success to his genius, it was common now for dissenters to complain that Lau had "ruined" Mayberry.

"Do you think I was wrong when I told him to watch the ball?" Lau retorted in an interview with the *Kansas City Star*'s Sid Bordman. "Was I wrong if I said use the whole field? Was I wrong when I said don't try to pull the outside pitch?" According to Mayberry fans: yes. The "powerless" Royals, they said, would never beat the home-run-hitting Yankees until Lau stopped meddling with his talent. Even among reporters who covered the team regularly, the Lau mystique proved fragile. "Lau is credited with being Brett's guru and making Brett what he is," a wire service reporter says. "I think that's bullshit. I wrote a story in 1976, when I was brand new to the beat, that made Lau sound like the Second Coming. God's gift to baseball." He shrugs. "But now I think you or I could have been George Brett's hitting instructor and he'd still be a great hitter." Or, as Mike McKenzie puts it, "It was a strength that George could talk to a guy about a mistake without being criticized or made to feel like a turd because he struck out. Lau was a guy he could *talk* to about striking out and why he did it. But to me, George Brett is the kid in the backyard. You throw him a sock and he hits it over the fence. You throw him a *golf* ball and he hits it over the fence. I think Charley Lau could have been John Jones or Freddie Nobody. . . . I still think George Brett would have been a great hitter."

"Nobody knows that," McRae retorts. "Everybody always says that about a good hitter, but that's cause people know nothing about hitting whatever. George's early training is the reason he's such a tremendous hitter. They pitch him away and he hits to left field, which most power hitters can't do. When they pitch him inside, he hits the home run."

Fred White tends to agree with McRae. "It's tempting to say George would have been a .350 hitter anyway. But how do you know? How many other guys have the ability to do that, but never get it unlocked?"

These were questions that Lau might have been able to answer, but he was rarely asked. "He didn't want anything to do with the media," testifies Doug Tucker, who says he endured a long, cold, silent spell from Lau. Even Lau's closest friends agreed that he was a sensitive,

154

extremely private person, easily inflamed by insult to his reputation or to the reputations of his friends. "He's intensely loyal," says a close friend. Outsiders interpreted Lau's manner as a frosty arrogance, and assumed that the Royals coach held all those outside the fraternal bond of baseballmen in profound contempt. Baseball writers, even veterans, tended to steer clear. Lau sat on a stool in front of his stall early every afternoon—right by the clubhouse door, where all the writers passed—and, with seeming great effort, pulled on his workout clothes, his eyes red, looking sleepy and grumpy and half a dozen other dwarfs. He spoke to the other coaches in dark whispers when he spoke at all. When approached by a stranger, he was devoid of smile or small talk and was given to long, stone-faced pauses when questioned. For Lau, speech itself seemed a great effort—lapsing into silence or a weary sigh—and he at times seemed about to terminate a conversation in midsentence. Most writers, expecting the "Svengali of Swat" to be a glib proselytizer of hitting theories, were unnerved. They moved on to Whitey Herzog's office. The Royals manager was blunt and funny and gave interviews that went off like little firecrackers. Lau, in contrast, talked as if he were afraid of betraying some sacred trust, and as if he resented being put in that position.

Lau had caught eleven years in the majors. He is powerfully built, with heavy legs, strong hands, lumberjack forearms and wrists. Lau's is the Hemingway masculinity, the kind most men don't feel they can measure up to. "The old fisherman type," one of the Royals explained, "the guy who spent his life on the seas with the wind blowin', out in the sun and the rain.

Weathered. The *stern* look, too. He doesn't waste words, but when he talks, you listen." And, like a Hemingway hero, emotionally stoic. "I think Charley holds a lot of his emotions in. He doesn't want people to know how he really feels."

"He's a very bashful person, really," says Fred White. An extended conversation with Charley Lau supports that view. In time, the abrupt answers elongate, the pauses become less painful, and Lau begins to volunteer information. The man that emerges is gentle, extraordinarily sentimental, and vulnerable. "His feelings for people run much deeper than the average," White says. "He can give himself totally to someone and dedicate himself to helping that person." It seemed ironic, then, that Lau's baseball reputation was based on hitting *mechanics*—on the hundreds of hours he had spent analyzing baseball swings on a videotape recorder at the Royals Baseball Academy in Sarasota, Florida; on ideas about body rhythms and tension, and launching position. Because when he talked about his players, he seemed most concerned with emotion. Confidence. Trust. *Fear.* Above all else, fear—for he encouraged his hitters to confess to their fears of being hit by a baseball, to their nightmare visions of cracked helmets and shattered jaws. Then he taught them how to overcome fear. He also understood pressure. "You have to understand," he said one afternoon in 1978, watching frustrated and disillusioned rookie Willie Wilson flail through batting practice with hands puffed up and bruised from switch-hitting lessons. "He's going through an orientation period which is the hardest thing a baseball player ever goes through," Lau said, barely speaking above a whisper. "The ability to cope with thirty thousand people, the big stadiums, the big-league atmosphere." He shrugged. "It may be phony, but it's there." To the press and the fans, Wilson was a punchless speed merchant of questionable future—immature, impatient, stubborn. To Lau, he was a twenty-two-year-old kid coping with new kinds of pressure. "People do different things to cope with it," Lau said. "Some people get quiet. Some people get loud." The danger with rookies was to expect too much of them, to demand maturity of performance before the maturing of the man. "Regardless of the ability they have," he said, "they're still twenty-year-old babies."

It was these qualities in Lau—the caring, the surprising warmth (startling, even, from such a forbidding-looking man), the sincerity—that inspired such devotion from players like McRae and Brett. Lau wasn't like most coaches, who praised players for their success, and shunned them in failure. "He was above that," one Royal remembers. "He was always there when you had a *bad* day. That's impressive. He was always there when it was *bad*."

It boiled down to patience. Charley Lau believed in it, counseled it, wrapped it like a cloak around the young Royal hitters. He was patient with them, and counseled them to be patient with themselves. Charley Lau personified the Royals approach.

It was a time, though, for fans to argue the merits of Yankee baseball versus Royals baseball. The Yankees swung for the fences; they struck out with the bases loaded; they hit grand slams; they lumbered around the bases; and they swaggered, as if the pinstripes still carried the sweat of Ruth, Gehrig, and DiMaggio. The Royals hit line drives, moved runners over with ground balls and bunts, stole bases, turned doubles into triples and outs into infield hits. Yankee fans demanded victory, *now*. Royals fans hoped to win, someday. The Yankees were owned by an impatient millionaire, the Royals by a patient millionaire. The Yankees *bought* their players: millions for Reggie Jackson, millions for Catfish Hunter, millions even for seldom used hurlers like Ken Holtzman and Don Gullett, millions for *any* established star—while bright prospects like Ron Guidry or Scott McGregor languished in the Yankee farm system. (The Yankees had no use for rookies.) The Royals *developed* their stars: amateur draft choices mostly, nurtured through seasons in Sarasota, Fort Myers, Jacksonville, and Omaha, molded in the image of Royals baseball, tailored to Royals stadium.

There was but one anomaly: the Royals manager, Dorrel "Whitey" Herzog. An impatient man.

To say that Herzog was a Yankee at heart would be unfair, for no man was more dedicated to beating the Bronx Bombers, and no man suffered more in dropping three straight championship series to the New Yorkers. But temperamentally, he was much closer to Yankees owner George Steinbrenner than he was to the Royals owner Ewing Kauffman. An admirer of Casey Stengel, Herzog liked the idea of a team that could batter its opponents into submission, as Stengel's Yankees had done to the teams Herzog played for in his eight-year major league playing career. The Royals, instead, nibbled away at opponents a run or two at a time, and usually endured nail-biting ninth innings before winning 4-3 or 3-1. It bothered Herzog that his future—portioned out in one-year contracts—lay in the hands of flaky and undependable bullpen rats, who made him look brilliant on Monday and stupid on Tuesday. It bothered him even more that the Royals refused to put their money into the free-agent market, where Steinbrenner was buying up all the goodies—the smoke-throwing relief pitchers, the twenty-game-winning hurlers, the left- and right-handed home run hitters that sat like bookends on the Yankee bench. He was too smart a baseball man to deny the importance of speed in vast Royals Stadium, but he also appreciated the value of power in the older, smaller ballparks of the American League. No sooner had Herzog peevishly dispatched John Mayberry, the only legitimate siege gun on the Royals, than he started bemoaning the lack of power in his remaining first basemen. Pete LaCock hit .303 for Herzog in 1977, .295 the following year, and .277 the year after that, but never won the everyday job at first because he couldn't hit more than five home runs a year. Catcher John Wathan, platooning with LaCock at first base, had seasons of .328 and .300, but he was a two-home-run-a-year man. Herzog loved Wathan on the bench as a pinch hitter—he called him "Cornfield" and used him in clutch situations—but he didn't want him as his first baseman. Herzog went so far, in 1979, as to trade for Mayberry's clone, veteran slugger George "Boomer" Scott, who, unhappily, hit no home runs (maybe it *was* the stadium?) and departed in a storm of ill will.

But what frustrated Herzog most of all was the knowledge that he had power hitters already, disguised as .330 hitters. Hal McRae could hit home runs. So could Amos Otis. Outfielder Al Cowens. And Brett? Herzog looked at New York's third baseman, Graig Nettles, who was lashing thirty homers a year into the short-right-field porch at Yankee Stadium, and judged that George Brett could do better. "I don't think that George realizes yet that he can be a Musial or a Mays or a Mantle," Herzog said. "He can hit .330 and still hit home runs. He's *strong*."

Herzog was not just thinking out loud. In 1977, under pressure from their manager, Brett and the other Royals warily went for the home run more often. The result? To everyone's surprise, the Royals exploded on the American League. Kansas City won 102 games, highlighted by a pennant run in which they were as hot as any team in history. They put together, starting in mid-August, winning streaks of seventeen, eleven, and nine games, and if a heartbreaking loss to the Yankees in the fifth game of the championship series had not shattered their illusions of omnipotence, the 1977 Royals might have lingered in baseball memories as one of the great teams. Knowledgeable fans, with the benefit of hindsight, will point out that Royals pitchers led the league in earned run average that year, but the striking difference in the Royals seemed to be the power in their bats. Hal McRae's batting average fell 34 points to .298, but he hit 21 home runs instead of 8 and drove in 92 runs instead 73. Darrell Porter hit 16 home runs, Amos Otis added 17. Al Cowens shocked everybody, soaring from 3 home runs to 23 home runs. And most telling of all, George Brett sacrificed 21 points from his .333 average of 1976, but jumped from 7 home runs to 22. Whitey Herzog had proved his point and Royals fans loved it: no more Punch and Judy. The Royals could hit with the big boys.

Or could they? The statistics moles, the people who revel in the dry-and-dusty numbers of baseball, began to unearth some curious figures early in the 1977 season. *Everybody,* it seemed, was hitting more home runs in 1977. Both leagues. Power teams and puny teams alike. The Boston Red Sox, who had led the league with 134 home runs in 1976, slugged *213* in 1977. The California Angels, the most powerless team in 1976, with only 63 home runs, smashed 131 a year later. The whole league's output jumped from 1122 homers to 2013; even allowing for expansion teams Seattle and Toronto, the increase was startling. Lowly Toronto, in fact, struck 100 home runs and tied for last in the league with Cleveland. In this light, the statisticians murmured, Kansas City's jump from 65 to 146 home runs suggested not a flowering of genuine power, but a symptom of some variable that was influencing the game as a whole. The culprit, it was offered, might be the ball itself; the Haitian women, who for years had been sewing up baseballs for the Spalding Company, had been displaced by new machines owned by Rawlings of St. Louis, which seemed to be producing rabbit balls. Players whose mightiest blows had previously fallen short of the warning track, suddenly were lining rockets around the foul pole or skying homers into somnolent bullpens.

"The ball is hopped up," Brett said.

Everybody had a theory as to *why* the new baseball was so hot—a different glue on the winding, a tighter bond with the cover, lack of soft spots on the ball. Hand-sewn stitches had made for loose covers, it was said, and therefore a deader ball. Professors at the University of Missouri at Rolla tested the balls for the American League. Their conclusion? The balls *were* livelier than before. Legal, but livelier. Sure enough, Rawlings tinkered with the machines in 1978, and home run production fell to pre-1977 levels. But by then, Whitey Herzog and the Royals were committed to a policy of home runs. Charley Lau's theories, it seemed, had fallen from favor in his own ballpark.

The most telling blow was struck at Royals Stadium on the afternoon of September 18, 1977, when a powerful-looking, brash, heroically named twenty-year-old rookie, Clint Hurdle, stepped into the box in the fifth inning against Seattle pitcher Glenn Abbott. Hurdle was the classic phenom—the American Association's Most Valuable Player and the one who replaced George Brett as the youngest player ever to see action in a Royals game. It was his first game in the big leagues, and the crowd seemed pleased with him just because of his build, his name, and his swagger, and because the Royals already seemed, to them, to be the best in baseball. But they were not prepared for what happened. The rookie ripped at an Abbott fastball: there was a solid crack and the ball rocketed deep toward right center field, going from white to black as it ascended from shadow into sunlight; plunging, finally, with an exultant splash into the back reaches of the water spectacular. The moment is curiously etched in the memories of most Royals fans, even those who were not there. Some blinked, some shook their heads in disbelief. George Brett's jaw dropped. As the rookie bounded around the bases with what proved to be the game-winning homer, the crowd cheered, then buzzed. Relief pitchers peered out the bullpen gates, trying to judge where the improbable blast had landed. In the Royals dugout, players and coaches pointed in amazement at the spot where the baseball had splashed so portentously.

They had no idea how big a splash.

"I shoulda hit a broken-bat single," Clint Hurdle said three years later. "A nice soft flare into center field." Hurdle, too, has that first home run etched in his memory, from a different perspective, of course—visible at first, then a blur, then a dark spot floating against the light towers. He alone remembers the *feel* of that ball jumping off the barrel of his bat, the solid, satisfying crunch that told him that he had connected, gotten it all. "That's the farthest ball I probably ever hit in my life!" Hurdle says, awe in his voice. "It was a *bomb!* Goddamn, my first game!" His voice drops. "It was too much."

It was enough to land Clint Hurdle on the cover of *Sports Illustrated* the following spring. Hurdle remembers a remark by the cynical, worldly center fielder, Amos Otis, shortly after they reported to the Royals training camp in Fort Myers. "Amos said, 'You don't have to worry. You made the club September eighteenth last year when you hit that ball out of the stadium. Whitey loves the long ball!'" Hurdle believes it. "That did it. Sure." He sees again the ball splashing so high and so far away, the fountain jets spurting triumphantly, the scoreboard erupting. "That lit up Whitey's eyes," Hurdle laughs. "Whitey probably thought I could do that *daily!*" So confident was Herzog that Hurdle was a wunderkind that he had encouraged Joe Burke to drop John Mayberry even if nothing could be gotten in return.

Burke had complied. Clint Hurdle—a twenty-year-old outfielder with nine major league games under his belt—was penciled in as the starting first baseman for a division-champion ball club, replacing a veteran slugger and gifted gloveman. The scene was set for a confrontation between the philosophies of patience and impatience: Charley Lau versus Whitey Herzog.

"The problem we had," Hurdle recalls, "was that there was no time for me to develop. With the moves Whitey had made, it was imperative for me to produce right away. There was no time for me to work on a weight shift, for example. It takes time. When Charley first got hold of George, it took him six weeks of 0-for-4s, 0-for-3s to get the hang of something." Hurdle didn't have that much time. The fans sensed immediately that he was lost at first base—unsure even of the boundaries, the wall, the railing, the dugout, the bag. He couldn't handle the skidding throws off the carpet that Mayberry had fielded so effortlessly. He chased pop-ups with a frantic desperation, risking crashes into the catcher and other infielders, but determined to make the plays anyway. He often didn't.

At the plate, Hurdle carried a double burden. He not only had to make up for his wretched fielding, he had to fulfill the promise of the magazine articles and the preseason hype, none of which were of his own making, however much he had reveled in the attention. The fans anticipated his every at bat with an ill-concealed eagerness: they viewed him as a human bomb, about to explode, destined to blast baseballs to the outer reaches beyond ballpark fences—just as he had that golden day in September. When the home runs failed to jump off his bat, they felt betrayed. They booed. They jeered. Some wrote scathing letters to the newspapers and ridiculed the youngster on the radio sports talk shows. "Clint had more pressure on him than anyone who's come to the big leagues in a long time," John Wathan recalls. "I could barely tie my shoes when I was nineteen years old, let alone play in the big leagues."

Charley Lau, the teacher, was unyielding. There were several fundamentals of the swing that every player *had* to master, he insisted, even if it meant, in the short run, looking foolish or ineffectual. In batting practice with Hurdle, Lau murmured praise when Hurdle grasped some elemental technique of the hands or stance—even if he missed the ball entirely. But Herzog, his ears starved for the staccato report of the bat on ball, watched Hurdle dribbling grounders toward shortstop with increasing exasperation. "I'd listen to Charley," Hurdle recalls. "But in the other ear I'd get my manager telling me to pull the ball, hit some home runs." When Hurdle tried to comply, to yank the ball over the fence, he struck out or popped up weakly. Charley Lau told him it was because he was trying to pull the ball. But when he went with the pitch and hit the ball to left, *Herzog* got upset. "Hell," Hurdle says, "I didn't know what the hell to do!"

The fans wrote Hurdle off as a big-headed youngster who was turning sullen because he wasn't as good as he had thought. "Clint was in a bad situation," Hal McRae says. "Caught between two people. And he wasn't mature enough or knowledgeable enough to know what worked best for him. He had no idea." Neither Herzog nor Lau was immune to criticism, either. Herzog had obviously made an error in thinking that Hurdle could replace Mayberry at first base: he acknowledged as much by late June, abandoning the experiment and relegating Hurdle to a part-time outfielder role. But few fans blamed Herzog for Hurdle's less-than-super hitting. Many of them shared Herzog's conviction that Hurdle was a "natural" hitter, the kind you leave alone—in Mike McKenzie's words, "the kid in the backyard—you throw him a sock and he hits it over the fence"—and his problems were probably due to Charley Lau's "tinkering." "If you tried to teach a bird the mechanics of flying," one press box onlooker said, "he'd end up with his beak in the ground and his tail feathers in the air." Even Lau's followers saw that Hurdle's mind was now too messed up to learn much from anybody. "Clint tried very hard to do what Charley taught," Wathan says, "but for some reason it just didn't work for him. Maybe he just wasn't ready yet to leave everything in Charley's hands."

As if the Hurdle situation weren't embarrassing enough, the rest of Lau's base seemed to be eroding. Nineteen seventy-eight was the year that the sore-shouldered McRae fell off to a .273 season, the year in which he stoically laid the blame for his slump on "bad mechanics"—which, unwittingly, put pressure on Lau to come up with a quick fix. George Brett, also hampered by injuries, fell below .300 for the first time since his rookie season, hitting .294. His home run production fell from 22 to 9. Al Cowens' turnaround seemed almost catastrophic: he dropped from .312 to .274, and from 23 home runs to 5. Almost to a man, Lau's students attributed their problems to home run fever, to their desire to recapture the euphoria of 1977, when those

Rawlings baseballs had floated out of ballparks like helium-filled balloons. "I'm not a power hitter," McRae shrugged. "It's ridiculous in this park to try to hit home runs when you weigh a hundred and eighty-five pounds, or a hundred and seventy-five, like Amos." In Cowens' case, his manager thought it was bad concentration at the plate, something to do with becoming a father for the first time and with his wife Velma's moving to Kansas City with the baby. "Maybe the baby was on my mind," Cowens said, unconvinced. "Babies and home runs." Cowens was now a tense hitter, an anxious hitter. He had an uncontrollable urge, he claimed, to hit home runs, to "shatter" baseballs. Instead, he found it difficult to move the ball out of the infield. "Every time I think home run," he murmured, "I mess up." Even the disciplined Brett said he was swinging too hard. "Finally, I've realized I don't have to go up there and swing for home runs," he said in June. All three claimed that they had been seduced by home run glamour. "For a while, we had a messed-up philosophy of hitting," McRae said, implying that they were now being punished, Old Testament style. Expelled from Lau's Garden of Eden. "You hit home runs by not trying to hit home runs," Lau told the *Star* in August. "I know that doesn't sound right, and it won't *read* right, but that's the way it is."

Herzog wasn't buying it. "I *do* think the ball is deader than it was last year," he conceded. "A year ago we had all those home runs up in the water spectacular. Balls were going out all over." But Herzog thought there was something more, a needless inhibition in his hitters.

"Clint might have been the last straw," Brett says. "We had guys who were capable of hitting home runs, but we weren't hitting 'em at all. Whitey was gung ho on Clint, and when he didn't have the year he expected, I think he blamed it on Charley."

Lau thought so, too. "I know I'm being criticized now," he said in September. "I get twenty letters a day to prove it."

One can look back on the 1978 season and marvel at the spell that Clint Hurdle's homer had thrown over the Royals, the ludicrous expectations it had engendered. Clint Hurdle's "flop" season produced a .264 average, 110 hits, 25 doubles, 5 triples, 7 home runs, and 56 RBIs. He was second on the Royals, behind Amos Otis, in game-winning RBIs with ten; he had a nine-game hitting streak in July; he tied the club's single-game record for RBIs when he drove in six against the Red Sox. His season, in fact, compared favorably with George Brett's rookie season, and was far superior to the rookie seasons of the other Royals starters. (His fellow rookie, Willie Wilson, hit .217 with no homers and 16 RBIs, but was not burdened with as much hype or responsibility, and blossomed the following year.) There was a sense, though, that Hurdle symbolized some sort of failure in the way the Royals went about things—some stodginess, some bureaucratic inertia that explained why the Royals lost to the Yankees every year in the championship series. "Here's a guy with tremendous potential," as Brett put it, "and he hadn't lived up to it yet." That's how Kansas City fans felt about their Royals. They were tired of hearing that the Royals were "building" a great club. And Whitey Herzog shared their impatience.

Still, it came as a shock on October 19, 1978, twelve days after the Royals season had ended on its third straight note of Yankee frustration, when Whitey Herzog announced that he did not intend to rehire one of his coaches for 1979. That coach was Charley Lau.

The outcry was instantaneous. A shaken Hal McRae went to the phone in his Bradenton, Florida, home, and dialed the *Star*'s sports desk in Kansas City. "A bad move," he said. "Definitely bad, and I don't like it. Next season we'll have a team of pull hitters, .240 hitters. Right now, I don't care if I come back to Kansas City or not. Somebody said he heard that Charley was getting a job with Seattle. I'll go *there* if they want me."

Frank White was less emotional, but the implications of the move did not escape him. "Seems like we're trying to change the philosophy of our club," he said.

George Brett, while privately heartsick, was publicly restrained. "The last time Charley got fired," he said, "Jack McKeon didn't like Charley and I didn't like Jack McKeon, so I did some blasting. But I've grown to respect Whitey Herzog as a man and as a manager, so I'm not going to blast him."

Royals general manager Joe Burke tried to maintain a dispassionate front. "Whitey feels Lau did a great job with some hitters and not so great with others," he told a press conference. "He just feels that one man can't teach fifty players to hit like each other." Sid Bordman's accounts in the *Star* suggested that there was more rancor involved. ("I guess he's my executive coach," he quoted Herzog. "My other coaches do the work and he watches.") But Herzog denied any ill will toward Lau. "I played with Charley in 1961, so he's a personal friend of mine. I *still* feel that he's a personal friend of mine." He added: "I'm not home run crazy. I know we've got a big ballpark, but I want our players to swing hard and get the ball into the outfield."

The suspicion lingered, among the Royals, that Herzog's firing of Lau had been motivated by the same protectiveness of authority that had spurred Jack McKeon. Herzog's stars had been under contract to a benign subcontractor who held the key to their loyalties and their performances. "That became one of the reasons for his leaving," Hurdle said later. "Charley became so close to the players that if they had problems, they went to *him*. Something happens, go to *Charley!*" Hurdle looked askance. "The manager doesn't like that! He likes to feel that he has control of the team. When he sees he's losing it, right before all the guys . . ." Hurdle shrugged.

"Baseball is such a head game," says Steve Busby. "You start to see things that aren't there and you get paranoid about your authority. It's a trap that we all fall into now and then. I imagine that if you were a manager and you felt that you were no longer in complete control, you'd have to try something to rectify it."

Fred White, the Royals broadcaster, found both Herzog and Lau reluctant to talk about the situation. "One night the subject came up," recalls White, who shared an apartment with Lau in 1978, "and we sat there and talked about it till three o'clock in the morning. And it came down to tears in his eyes. It came down to crying, to be honest. But he would never say exactly what it was and he would never say, 'I'm gonna straighten it out.' All he would say was, 'This ball club is my whole life and I wanna stay here.'

"And I said, 'Why don't you go talk to him and straighten it out?'

"He said, 'I can't.'

"He had such a strong sense of honor. Whatever it was between him and Whitey . . . he felt it wasn't anybody else's business and he wasn't gonna talk about it. It was obvious that it was gnawin' at him. He wanted so badly to stay here. But he just wouldn't go and say, 'I'm wrong.' He was never gonna change the way he approached players, and he was never gonna change his theory of hitting."

And so, after seven and one-half years, Lau was no longer a Royal. At a press conference in New York, on October 25, 1978, it was announced that Charley Lau had signed a contract to be hitting instructor for a new team.

The New York Yankees.

"At first I thought, Jesus Christ, I can't hit without Charley."

That's how George Brett approached the 1979 season. It was a constant refrain, paraphrased and restated with great ingenuity. Doug Tucker remembers Brett brooding about the loss of Charley Lau with the line, "I'm like a baby whose been breast-fed all my life, and now they're gonna put me on the bottle." Brett had no reason to panic—he was an established star with a .305 lifetime average—but the old misgivings emerged. He feared that he would not hit, that he was merely an extension of Lau's baseball intellect. "Every big-league hitter is very insecure," Lau explained later, "and I had tried to do some of George's thinking for him. He relied on me. And when I wasn't there, he suddenly had to do it himself." Brett couldn't shake the memory of the *first* time Lau had been fired, in 1974, and how he had gone hitless in his last three games. "They took away the man that made me hit," he had said of that brief trial. "They" had done it again.

Of equal concern to Brett, when he reported to spring training, was the woeful condition of his chronically brittle right thumb. For several seasons, a bone chip had tormented Brett; then, before the 1979 season, in an overzealous scramble for a loose ball in a charity basketball game, he had broken the thumb. It was expected to heal in time for spring training, but doctors later decided that the bone chip had to go. The subsequent operation limited Brett's spring training to interviews under the palm trees and shagging ground balls with his glove hand. His right hand turned pale under bandages and a cast.

Hal McRae wasn't much better off. His scarred shoulder testified to off-season rotator cuff surgery, and the lengthy workouts brought pain and stiffness. When he first started taking batting practice, the Royals gathered around the cage, wincing at every swing, but exulting at the modest line drives that sprang from his bat. McRae could not, however, swing hard, and once committed he dared not check his swing; he spun around instead, grinning sheepishly. For once, Whitey Herzog could not join in the usual spring training optimism. If watching sore-armed shortstop Fred Patek bounce throw after throw to first base made Herzog apprehensive about the upcoming season, the prospect of playing without a healthy Brett and McRae was positively maudlin.

When the Yanks came to play the Royals at Terry Park in Fort Myers, their new, granite-faced hitting coach almost had to fight off the Royals who gathered around him—to the amusement of veteran Yankees like Reggie Jackson, who teased Lau about his "children." Lau had words of encouragement for Brett and McRae, but he responded to specific questions in generalities and noncommittal grunts. Their mentor was wearing pinstripes now, not Royal blue. "They had a helluva code of honor now that Charley was with the Yankees," Fred White says. "George didn't want to put Charley in the position that somebody on the Yankees would think that he was helping George."

There wasn't, of course, much advice that Lau could have offered Brett and McRae anyhow; his theories didn't allow for broken thumbs and postsurgical shoulders. Talk centered, rather, on what role Lau would play on the Yankees, a team not noted for patience or continuity on its coaching staff. Unlike the Royals, there were few youngsters on the Yankees to coach, and the veterans were mostly accomplished and set in their ways. Reggie Jackson and Graig Nettles, it was assumed, would continue to blast away at Yankee Stadium's short-right-field porch, regardless of Lau's all-fields philosophy, and star catcher Thurman Munson (as taciturn as Lau, but without the warmth) seemed an unlikely candidate for hitting lessons. The Royals joked that Lou Piniella's dream had finally been realized: he would have Charley Lau as his exclusive hitting coach.

In Kansas City, Brett and McRae were left with each other, and their confidence seemed to rush out the missing side of The Triangle. "After a four- or five-year period we had learned to think like Charley," McRae says, "but we were still afraid of being away from him. We figured we'd still be good hitters . . . but we weren't sure. For about four years, with Charley, the game was fairly easy. He was calling the pitches, telling us what to look for. And it was fun. We always knew we were gonna get a couple of hits when we came to the park, and we started hitting the ball where we *wanted* to hit it. I started telling guys on the bench where I was gonna hit the ball. I'd hit the ball a couple of months to left, then I'd hit it a couple of months to right." He shrugs. "But without Charley . . . we just weren't sure."

For the Royals, the first series of the 1979 season was heartening—they swept three games from Toronto—but their opening-game victory, 11-2, was played in a frigid Kansas City windstorm that drove almost all of the 37,704 fans out of the stadium minutes after the Royals exploded for nine runs in the first two innings. Brett's thumb bothered him more in cold weather, so the polar blast was ominous. "The first month is so *damn* cold," he said. "If you don't hit the ball right, it *stings*." Later, recalling his punchless hitting in April and May, he admitted that the injury had robbed him of his aggressiveness. "One of the reasons that I got off to such a slow start wasn't the lack of spring training," he said. "I was *scared*. I was scared of the pain I'd feel if I didn't hit the ball right. I was feeling for the ball instead of being aggressive, instead of trying to break the ball in half when I swung."

The bad thumb not only inhibited Brett's hitting, it also obscured the progress he had made as a fielder. The fans' signs reading HARD-HAT-AREA had come down over the years as Brett had conquered his scatter-armed tendencies, but they went up again in the spring of 1979, as the bandages and the pain forced Brett to play third as though he had gloves on *both* hands. He committed thirty-one errors in 1979, but he points out, "I probably made eighteen or twenty of them the first two months of the season."

Brett was impatient with those who thought he had been stupid to break his finger in the first place, particularly in a charity basketball game. "What the hell do you expect me to do?" he asked. "I can't stay in my house all winter and get in shape."

There were other means of exercise, his critics persisted, less dangerous than basketball with its toll of broken fingers, sprained ankles, and shredded knees. Had Brett considered racquetball?

"Racquetball?" he snorted. "Tom Poquette tore apart his knee playing racquetball. And how many people do you read about slipping and falling in the snow?" Brett warmed to the subject. "I know a guy back in California who walked into the kitchen table, slipped on a piece of waxed paper, and tore the ligaments in his knee! You can get hurt doing *anything*." He began to mutter. "Last night I had a fire. Coulda got my hand caught in it and burned the damn thing off. . . ."

Brett's fatalism, his teammates knew, was not the product of philosophy courses, but of a compulsive restlessness, an inability to tolerate inactivity. John Wathan recalled another Brett injury when they were both youngsters playing for the Royals San Jose farm club. "He broke his foot that year and had a cast on it up to his knee," Wathan said. "So they decided to send him home to El Segundo to recuperate. But George could never sit still, he always wants to compete at something. So he was out playing basketball with his cast on"—

Wathan laughed—"and he broke his cast. So he had to have the foot re-X-rayed in El Segundo. And as it turned out, either the break wasn't as bad as they first thought, or the doctor diagnosed it poorly the first time. They said they couldn't find anything wrong with it. So George came back and started playing again right away."

Prudence, obviously, was alien to George Brett's character. Several times a year he would hurl himself upon some dugout roof in pursuit of a foul pop-up, trusting in Providence to protect his spine, skull, and ribs from disabling injury. Just as often he tumbled over the box seats railing, his rear end poking skyward, his nose pressed on a concrete step smelling of popcorn, feet, and spilled beer. "Who knows?" he would grin. "If you fall in the stands you might meet a good-looking girl. That's just the way I play baseball. I have fun."

Only suddenly it *wasn't* fun. "Anything with the hand," he explained later. "I mean, when I separated my shoulder, I could still play with that. But I've had some bad bone bruises on my glove hand, and no matter where you catch the ball you can feel it. And with this, my thumb was really sensitive. I had tape all around the damn thing and it was really hard to get a good grip. The ball didn't feel right." Curiously, at the plate the pain coursed through Brett's thumb only when he swung and missed. "When I *hit* the ball," he explained, "I take my top hand off. When I don't hit the ball—" He gripped an imaginary bat and rolled his wrists over. "—I kinda come down on the damn thing like this."

Brett began to brood. He fretted over the absence of Charley Lau. He worried about his swollen hand. And—by his standards at least—he quit hustling. "It'll be just

about the time when you want to say somethin' to him,"
Clint Hurdle says, "like, 'Hey! Get your head out of your
butt.' But before you do"—Hurdle laughs—"he's already
done it. He's already turned it around."

"A lot of it was in my head," Brett admits. Partly it
was the thumb, but partly it was the separation from
Charley Lau, and it took Brett time to accept that he had
learned from Lau, that Charley had not been a puppet-
master pulling his strings, but an effective teacher. "As
the season progressed," Brett says, "I started remembering more and more of the things he taught me." When
memory failed, Brett still had Hal McRae to compare
notes with; and for all McRae's protestations that life
without Lau was unbearable, McRae in some ways
replaced Lau for the younger Royals. He had absorbed
most of Lau's theories and, like Lau, he was a man whom
players could talk to about personal problems, their
fears and misgivings. "I guess I just talk all the time,"
McRae laughed, dismissing the idea that he was a
leader. "Sometimes I see an opportunity to maybe say
something to a guy that might help, but sometimes I
won't say anything. During the course of a season or a
game, I'm kinda moody. I have to worry about *myself,*
too." The fact remained that both Brett and McRae had
matured as hitters. McRae's progress was hampered by
the severity of his shoulder injury—he finally put himself on the disabled list to allow the joint to heal from the
surgery—but his .288, with 10 homers and 74 RBIs in
only 393 at bats, proved that he could cope without Lau
actually at his elbow. Brett's progress, once his thumb
had healed, was even more spectacular. He led the
league in hits with 212 and triples with 20, belted 23

homers, scored 119 runs, and had his first 100 RBI season with 107. He struck out only 36 times and stole 17 bases. And his average jumped back up to .329. For the first time, Brett's name began to be mentioned in the tight constellation of baseball's most regarded players: Dave Parker, Pete Rose, Reggie Jackson, Fred Lynn. . . . "I think George is now the best player in the league by far," Whitey Herzog said. Having finally combined a season of power and high average, Brett entered negotiations for an extension of his contract—not a renegotiation, the Royals insisted—from a position of strength, the specter of free agency dangling like a sword over Joe Burke, who knew well the crucial role Brett played in the establishment of a lasting Royals tradition in Kansas City. In turn, daydreaming Yankee fans—mindful of George Steinbrenner's bountiful purse and acquisitive eye for star talent—speculated that a George Brett in pinstripes might rewrite the record books. (The same speculation had centered on other stars in the past—Ted Williams, in particular, with his power to right field. Wasn't there the danger, Charley Lau was asked, that even a great hitter like Brett might disturb his hitting mechanics trying to pull everything for home runs? "Damn right," Lau said. "But George can analyze himself and he knows the pitfalls, what pulling can do to him. The minute it doesn't work, he'll back off the plate and square up again. He's very aware of what happens during his swing.")

Brett steadfastly denied, however, that he yearned for brighter lights and big cities. "I don't want to move to New York," he said at his home one afternoon, contemplating the next day's negotiating session with Joe

Burke and Ewing Kauffman. "I don't want to move to California. I don't want to move to Milwaukee. I like it here. I'm sure I could go somewhere and make more money than I will playing for the Royals, but I'm not gonna look back." He stretched his legs out and leaned back on his couch. "I hate to use the word 'family.' I think the Pittsburgh Pirates have a patent on that. But the Royals have treated me like family. So I'm not going to storm in there with an agent. I'm going in there myself. There's really no reason to leave if we can be fair with each other."

Unlike several other Royals starters, who had signed long-term contracts which, in light of escalating player salaries, they later regarded as fools' pacts, Brett expressed no resentment over his existing contract and refused to second-guess himself. "When I signed my last contract in seventy-six I thought, God damn, Jesus! This is unbelievable!" His eyes got wide. "I'm twenty-two, twenty-three years old with all this money! What the hell am I gonna do?" His smile faded. "The big thing I wanted then was security. I wanted some deferred money in case something happened to me, like if I broke both legs in a car accident and couldn't play anymore. I've been told I should have signed a three-year contract instead of a five, but who was to know what would happen?" He shrugged. "I got more money. More money, more security. I'm in the same boat now. I want security. But I don't think I'm gonna defer any because I've already deferred a lot."

The day before, Brett said, he had conferred with financial consultant Mike Herman, who had helped him rough out a contract proposal to show the Royals. "Mike said, 'What do you want? How much do you really need to live on?'" Brett seemed to ponder how much he spent a month on toothpaste, laundry, and blue jeans. "I said, 'It's not a question of what I need to live on. I want to be fair to myself compared to what other people in my profession are making.'

"So we talked and came up to a figure. I said, 'Be honest with me, Mike. Am I asking too high?' And he says, 'No. I think it's a very fair figure.' I said, 'Jesus Christ, what happens if I go in there and say, 'Mr. Kauffman, Mr. Burke, this is what I want'—they're gonna shit in their pants!'"

Herman thought not. After all, hadn't Brett in 1976 shown up for negotiations with a figure in mind, only to have Kauffman and Burke *top* it on their first offer? Brett nodded and then laughed, embarrassed. "I don't think they'll do it this time."

Brett shook his head. "Mike advised me. He said, 'George, I'm the best there is in the world.' And I believe him! Mike is the best handler of big bucks of anybody in the world. He *knows*. He told me, 'I want you to get a good tax guy and a good lawyer. Not an agent! Pay them by the hour.'" Brett held up one finger. "'I'll let the tax guy look at all my records. All the things I own, the things I don't own, the things that maybe I *should* own. *Okay, if we get so much money, I think we should structure it this way.*" Brett held up two fingers. "The lawyer will read the contract and talk to me in my own language so I'll know what's in it. Mr. Kauffman, Mr. Burke, and Mike—their language is high financial, the book of law. I need somebody I can trust who will come over to my home and say, 'This is what they offered you.'

Take a couple of hours and go over everything." He
cocked his head to one side. "'Cause the last contract, I
didn't. My contract is very basic, but I really don't
understand some things."

There was one sobering fact for Brett to consider: that
the Royals, operating in one of the smallest markets in
professional sports, could hardly be expected to match
greenbacks with George Steinbrenner, Ted Turner, and
Gene Autry, the team owners most often accused of
distorting baseball salary structures with their benefi-
cence. "Teams like Kansas City just don't have the TV
revenues of a New York," Brett conceded. "We get five
hundred thousand. They get what? Twenty million?" He
snorted. "The Yankees could have ten people come to the
stadium next year and still make money. We have to
rely on attendance to make money." The clearest remedy
for this competitive handicap, Brett offered, was a
stronger compensation rule for the signing of free
agents—a remedy bitterly opposed by the Major League
Baseball Players Association. "They're gonna *have* to
come up with some kind of rule like football's Rozelle
Rule," Brett said, referring to football's free-agent compensation system. "Basketball's done it, football's done
it, baseball's gonna be next. Because the salaries *are*
getting outrageous. If George Brett plays out his option,
or somebody making over a hundred thousand a year
plays out his option, you gotta give up, what? A starting
ballplayer? And a first-round draft choice or two minor
league players? Whatever. *Then,* people are gonna be a
little more reluctant to sign people." That prospect, of a
moribund free-agent market—so horrifying to the
MLBPA and its executive director Marvin Miller—did

not seem to alarm Brett. "It can't keep going like it has. It's impossible."

He looked out the window and smiled to himself. "I *was* gonna go play basketball today. But I can't go in there tomorrow with my arm in a sling, my finger in a cast, a black eye. They'll think, This guy's more risky than we thought."

He was not getting cautious, his look said—just practical. "I'm gonna go in tomorrow and I'm gonna *listen*. There's a little bit of risk involved. If I play out the remaining two years of my contract, I might have two bad years. My value might go down a little bit. And I think that the same time I play out my option, Mike Schmidt [Phillies third baseman] will play out his. Which could cause some problems for me, cause Mike Schmidt is a hell of a ballplayer." He shrugged. "The compensation rule might come in." He continued to stare out the window. "I don't want to look back and say, 'I shoulda done this or I shoulda done that.'"

He added, softly, "I don't want the world."

Other Royals had strong years in 1979. Amos Otis, who conducted a sharp war of words with Whitey Herzog through the media, had his best season in years, hitting .295 with 18 homers and 90 RBIs. Willie Wilson, seizing an outfield spot after Al Cowens' jaw was shattered by an Ed Farmer fastball in Arlington, Texas, hit .315 and rattled pitchers with 83 stolen bases and 5 inside-the-park home runs. Intense, bespectacled catcher Darrell Porter hit a powerful .291, smashed 20 homers and drove in 112. Herzog's dispatching of Charley Lau, clearly, was no longer an issue with the fans.

Herzog himself was, though. The pitching staff that had served him so capably through four winning seasons and three straight Western Division titles suddenly deserted Herzog in 1979; the fans, characteristically, blamed the manager. Blinded by the prevailing notion that a manager's skill is revealed mostly by his use of pinch hitters and relief pitchers, Herzog's critics assailed his "predictability" and his penchant for playing the percentages. Except for the obvious contempt he showed toward obscene correspondents and the people who questioned his intelligence and· character in the letters column of the *Kansas City Times,* he took the criticism with relatively good humor. He dismissed it as the handiwork of half-wits and sports dilettantes. "Only crackpots write in," he said one night, putting his stockinged feet up on his desk in the classic managerial posture. "I think it's terrible when a newspaper prints something like that. They don't understand that I am a human being. I have kids growing up, and they read that bullshit." The fans, he said, hated to hear the truth. "You can't win without a bullpen. If your bullpen is good and your people are playing good, then you're a smart manager. When your bullpen is bad, you become dumb.

"I came in here at a pretty good time," Herzog said, reflecting on the chaotic, unhappy bunch of Royals he had inherited from Jack McKeon in 1975. "The club was struggling, but they probably had a better ballclub than they showed up to that time. When I came they were trying to close out ball games with Lindy McDaniel, and he was getting up in age"—Herzog winked—"and his slider was getting up too. It just so happened that later we got a little left-hand-right-hand balance that helped our pitching staff and we had two guys on the bench who weren't playing—Frank White and Al Cowens." Herzog clasped his hands behind his head and looked reflective. "If I ever did anything here, it's the fact I put those two guys in the lineup, against the wishes of a lot of people. And they became super ballplayers." He snorted. "You have to know talent, there's no doubt about it. It's easy to manage when you have guys you know are gonna give you one hundred percent every day, and who play on the same level so you know about what to expect from them."

Expectations, of course, had been the bane of Herzog's great gamble, Clint Hurdle, who was demoted to the Omaha Royals in 1979, consigned to weeks of angry ineffectuality under the dimmer lights of American Association ballparks. Perhaps Herzog was thinking of Hurdle when he said, "I think the most dangerous thing a manager can do is to expect too much from a player. Some guys you can hit-and-run with, some guys you can't. Some guys, you don't even *ask* 'em to bunt, because they can't. You just gotta let them play their game."

Herzog summed up in a burst of Stengelese: "A player can't do anything he can't do." He mussed his sandy hair and wiggled his toes. "Other guys can do everything you want."

A six-game win streak put the Royals at 42-33 on June 28, 1979, in a first-place tie with the California Angels. But the Royals July was reminiscent of those bittersweet martyred summers of Kansas City's baseball past, devoted to the extravagant losing binges of the Kansas City A's. The Royals lost seven straight games (which shocked the faithful) and then won one. When they lost seven more in a row, making it fourteen out of fifteen, shrill voices complained that the Royals conservative policies had gone bankrupt. Kauffman and Burke had pinched too many pennies, spurned too many free agents, sucked the farm system dry. Ironically, one of those shrill voices belonged to Whitey Herzog, who was outspoken in his disapproval of the Royals personnel policies—particularly of Joe Burke's inability to swing trades for players Herzog coveted. When it was learned that Burke and Kauffman had warned Herzog to confine his criticisms to the proper organizational forums—that is, to button his lip—a tide of sympathy swung in Herzog's direction. Above all else, baseball fans loved straight talk, and Herzog was a dangerously candid man. Burke's assertion that a baseball manager should be a good "organization man" cast Herzog in the role of sharp-tongued, blue-collared Everyman, puncturing the self-serving obfuscations of thin-lipped, necktied corporate drones. If it came to a choice, baseball fans preferred Whitey—with his boyish charm and roughhouse talk—to Joe Burke with his State Department stiffness and Grim Reaper pronouncements.

The antagonism sometimes spilled over in public. One night, in the press club at Royals Stadium, Ewing Kauffman loudly second-guessed Herzog for pinch-hitting for Frank White in the late innings of a just-completed Royals victory, grumbling, "You don't take the best second baseman in baseball out of the game!" When Herzog ambled in for a postgame drink, freshly showered, in golf slacks and a sweater, Kauffman, red-faced, chewed him out in front of a table full of cronies—

until Herzog, smiling stiffly, turned and walked away from the still-lecturing owner. Those in attendance took it for granted that Herzog's days were numbered, that it was merely a question of who would bleed the most when the cutting took place.

Sadly, at the same time Herzog's stock with the fans rose, it was falling in the clubhouse. As a late bid to catch the Angels fell short, players found reasons to question Herzog's policies, or to unearth old grievances in ways that eroded the manager's authority. Several of the black players were still disenchanted over the John Mayberry fiasco of 1977, insisting that Herzog had hustled off that supposedly vital cog in the Royals machine in a mere fit of pique. Charley Lau's friends continued to grieve over *his* departure. Still others grumbled about their playing time—the prime preoccupation on a losing ball club. Herzog became an issue to be argued, pro or con, like fluoridation or gun control. "You have those that are for, and those that are against," as Frank White put it, "and those that are just *there*." White put himself in the third category, but he admitted later that Herzog had done things in 1979 that even *he* questioned. "One got the feeling that he felt insecure in his job and it affected the managerial aspects of the game. He lost the respect of a lot of players, something that he had *had* in previous seasons."

From Hal McRae, battling to recapture his health and his lost hitting stroke, questions about managers and authority elicited some surprising answers. "To get in twenty years," he said, referring to his baseball pension, "I'd have to coach. But I wouldn't like to manage." He sat down on the stool in front of his locker and surveyed the clubhouse with amusement. "I couldn't deal with these young players today. In order for me to manage the way I'd want to manage, I'd have to be about six-four and about two-forty." He giggled. "They'd either do it my way, or that's *it,* let's go in the tunnel and fight." The brawling manager was an anachronism, McRae knew, lingering only in the confused psyche of Billy Martin. But McRae's model manager was still around in the person of Don Zimmer, the short, pudgy Red Sox pilot who had been McRae's manager in the minor leagues. Not that Zimmer actually hit players, or grabbed them by the shoulders and shook them until their fillings fell out. "But you always felt he *could,*" McRae said admiringly. "The way he screamed, the way his eyes got big!"

Reconciling McRae's ideal manager with his beloved coach—the tight-lipped, reclusive Charley Lau—was not easy. But nothing about the Royals seemed easy at the end of the 1979 season. When, as expected, Whitey Herzog was not offered another one-year contract, it seemed as if the Royals dreams of a World Series had burst. Their most successful manager was banished to the russet hills of autumn, with shotgun and dog. The entire coaching staff was dismissed. The pitching staff was in shambles, the bullpen seemed bare. Clint Hurdle was a potential embarrassment, a player "ruined," it was said, by Herzog or Lau or Burke or whomever—at the age of twenty-two. With both Lau and Herzog gone, it was not even certain which philosophy had finally won: impatience or patience?

Amid all this doubt and confusion, George Brett stood out. He was the francise. And if he suddenly felt the need for a lake retreat, a more private life, and for a more disciplined life-style, it was little wonder. His moorings had pulled loose: no more Charley Lau to pat him on the back, no more Whitey Herzog to kick him in the butt. And possibly no more Hal McRae, whose future as a Royal—as a ballplayer, even—was now in question.

It must have come as a shock. The pecking order had thinned out, and George Brett was needed now at the top.

Would he respond? "The thing that intrigues me about him" one newsman reflected, "is that he has no desire to be a leader. He isn't even intrigued by it. He doesn't want to be a Pete Rose. He says, 'I just wanta go play ball. Play hard.'" The newsman shook his head. "Brett will never be the guy saying, 'I can lead you to the pennant.'"

In the stillness of his Lake Quivira chalet, George Brett stared at the two-year-old copy of *Sports Illustrated* on his coffee table—the cover with the magical rookie in royal blue reaching for stardom, trying to duplicate his September blast—and cocked his head. "If Clint has a bad year," he said coolly, "I'm taking this off the table."

Then he guffawed.

George Brett was ready. He was already psyching down.

PART THREE

PSYCHING DOWN

1. Animal House

It had never rained so hard.

The clouds gathering to the south and west had piled up like a black wall. Oakland's Matt Keough walked Brett with two out in the bottom of the first, but he was no further than 1-and-1 on Al Cowens when rain began to pelt the stadium. The air turned gray and the players were already drenched before the home-plate umpire could wave them into the dugout. Umbrellas broke out in the stands, but most of the fans scrambled back under the upper decks to watch George Toma's ground crew unfurl the royal blue tarpaulin, which whipped wildly in the wind. Great waves swept across its surface as the dripping youngsters tried to subdue it, anchoring the edges with weights while wind bubbles boiled in it, shoulder high and higher, around the mound. Water cascaded down the grandstand steps and gushed into the dugouts. Small children scampered and splashed around; several actually swam in the field-level boxes. From the press box, the giant scoreboard was temporarily invisible, lost in the deluge. From the stadium rim, the lights of nearby Arrowhead Stadium, across the parking lot, seemed to descend, as gale winds flung sheets of wind skyward.

Few sensed the imminent danger. Not, at least, until they tried to leave the stadium by certain low-lying roads, which were turning into rivers. The Kansas City Chiefs head football coach, Paul Wiggin, leaving Arrowhead after working late, had his car stall in high water near Manchester Trafficway and Highway 40. As the water rose around him, the alarmed Wiggin was forced to climb out the window and sit on his roof, waiting for help. "It makes you realize," he said later, "how insignificant football really is." Only when the rain abated momentarily, and he saw lights nearby, did Wiggin judge it prudent to wade to high ground and safety.

Others were not so fortunate. Several died in the network of narrow, wooded roads that encircled the Truman Sports Complex. It was the night of Monday, September 12, 1977, and before midnight, twenty-five Kansas Citians were to die in flash floods: drivers seized by rampaging Brush Creek, children drowned in underground garages, gawkers caught in the very surge of brown water that had drawn them out of their homes. Hundreds were to be left homeless, old neighborhoods devastated. A two-block-wide strip through the posh Country Club Plaza was to be demolished: abandoned cars hurtling through plate-glass windows; antiques, muddy books, and bolts of costly fabrics tumbling and bobbing through the streets; trees crashing into hotel ballrooms.

But that would come later in the evening. In the Royals clubhouse the atmosphere was playful. For one thing, the team was in first place, riding a twelve-game winning streak, and playing the best baseball in its history. For another, the rainout promised a free evening. For George Brett, the hour's delay until the game was officially called afforded time for a prank to grow in his fertile brain. He had a score to settle, it seemed, with a twenty-nine-year-old stripper named Morganna, "The Wild One"—known more recently as "Baseball's Kissing Bandit." Three weeks before, during a game, the top-heavy stripper had vaulted the left-field fence, bounced across the outfield in hot pants and a tight jersey, and pursued a seemingly bashful Brett across the infield, to the delight of a raucous and cheering crowd. "Kiss me quick," she had said. "Kansas City sent me." Finally relenting, Brett had let her plant a wet one on his cheek, to another cheer. Blushing security officers and police had then led the bounteous intruder off the field and ultimately to jail. A Wirephoto—of the 45-23-39 Morganna, on tiptoe, trying to surmount her own anatomy to reward the gallant knight with the bat in his hand—had made papers across the country. A similar shot—of Morganna kissing the towering Milwaukee coach, Frank Howard—was allegedly displayed at the Baseball Hall of Fame in Cooperstown, New York. "That's the only way you'll ever get *your* foot in the Hall of Fame," Brett's teammates razzed.

Brett had vowed revenge, and now, with the rainout,

he had a plan. Making a phone call to the riverfront burlesque house where Morganna was performing, he warned the management that he was on his way. Then he recruited two Royals pitchers for his entourage, Andy Hassler and Doug Bird. Associated Press photographer John Philo, privy to the plot, tipped off AP writer Dan George, who was covering the game, and the raiding party was complete.

Oblivious to the tragedy unfolding in the southern parts of the city, the raiders, in two cars, drove through the blinding rain on Interstate 70, working their way toward a small movie house in a warehouse district known as River Quay. This riverfront neighborhood, at the foot of the downtown bluffs, had been developing a reputation for restaurants and nightlife until local mobsters started settling beefs by torching each other's clubs and by stuffing dead people into trunks of cars. Now, this bombed-out and boarded-up battle zone housed only one establishment of citywide reputation: the Old Chelsea Theatre, purveyor of porno double features and live stage shows.

Philo and Dan George reached the theater first and interviewed Morganna, but as show time approached she apologized and withdrew to make her preparations. The first dancer was already on the runway, gyrating to a record, when the three Royals arrived, dripping and laughing in the lobby. "Hassler was embarrassed to be there," Dan George remembers, "and the sight of a wire service photographer unnerved him." "Don't say I'm here," he implored George. "My wife will kill me!" That promise secured, the five men pushed through the curtained entry into the darkened theater, which was about one third filled—finding seats in one of the back rows, at a respectable distance from the pastel-lighted flesh writhing on the stage.

"Bird's got a degenerate look about him anyway," laughs George, explaining what happened next. Brett and Bird decided to sit closer to the runway, and Bird, in his eagerness, took the most direct route, falling over seats and causing a commotion. Hassler, rooted in his seat at the back, blanched. "If he'd had an overcoat and a slouch hat," George says, "he'd have had it on."

When Morganna torched her way into the spotlight, the audience whistled and hooted. She had shed only a red hat and a feather boa when Brett vaulted onto the runway, to the delight of the sparse crowd, and returned the stolen kiss. "Now we're even," he said. Then he donned the floppy red hat, wrapped the feather boa around his neck, and posed for Philo's camera with Morganna clinging to his arm.

A new George Brett was born.

The old George Brett? "I really don't know," he says, trying to explain how he had been tagged the "all-American Boy" in his early seasons as a Royal. "When I was a rookie here, I was the new kid in town. I had the blond hair, I was from California. People thought I was kinda different." Women of all ages took an immediate interest in his progress—not just teenage girls who swooned and called him a "hunk," but grandmothers, as well, who wanted to bake him cupcakes and knit him mittens. "He has an impish smile," a woman sportswriter divined years later, "that gives him the look of a wayward altar boy. . . ." He was, of course, not quite drinking age, but he was intoxicated with the possibilities of adulthood, with his independence and sudden affluence.

You can trace George Brett's baseball fortunes through the houses he's owned in Kansas City. He acquired his first mortgage in 1974. Royals pitcher Paul Splittorff, a part-time realtor, showed him around a treeless subdivision in Blue Springs, Missouri, a few miles east of Royals Stadium. Many of the married players had bought houses there, in the $40,000–$50,000 range, and Brett, like a sailor selecting a berth, said, "I'll take it," the first day of house hunting. (According to his father, "George thought, Geez, that'd be nice, I'd have my own house! So he bought a house!") He apparently didn't notice that his new neighborhood lacked sidewalks or streetlights, and no one told him that the nightlife for a bachelor, in Blue Springs, consisted of watching TV while a dog barked in somebody's yard down the street.

Charley Lau recalls a time, shortly after Brett moved into his new house, when the phone rang late at night. "George said, 'Hey, Lau, come out here, I'm scared.'" There were no intruders jimmying Brett's windows, just that heavy quiet that blankets the suburbs when the tricycles and skateboards have been shut away for the night. "He was a homesick boy, scared of the dark," Lau says. "He didn't wanta stay in the house by himself. I told that to my wife, and she said, 'Well—he's human, too, isn't he?'"

To ward off the jitters and the loneliness, Brett got into the habit of eating out. He paid frequent visits to the houses of players who lived within a few blocks of him, like Splittorff, Fred Patek, and Doug Bird. "I didn't know Kansas City at all," Brett says. "I'd go to some Mexican restaurant out in Blue Springs, I don't remember the name of it—Bulls Eye Inn or something." He shrugs. "And then I'd go to bed."

Meanwhile, in Omaha, another young third baseman, already a good friend of Brett's, was making a similar impression on Midwest sensibilities. Jamie Quirk was a tall, handsome youngster—like Brett, a blond, California surfer prototype—who had recently captured the most fan ballots as "Omaha's Most Popular Player." At twenty, Quirk had batted .274 for the Triple A club, with 13 home runs and 64 runs batted in, figures almost identical to Brett's Omaha record. "We were basically competing with each other," Quirk recalls, "but George was always a level ahead of me, and I never looked at it like he was keeping me from making the major leagues. If you hit, they'll find a place for you to play. But I knew all along that as soon as I made the club they were gonna move me from third base. I never threatened George's position at all." Since Quirk was a bachelor, too, and a good friend, Brett made him a houseguest in September 1975, when the Royals gave Quirk his first taste of the big leagues. The following spring, when Quirk made the team, Brett became his landlord, housemate, and constant companion. The so-called "Bobbsey Twins" were born. "They were inseparable," one of the Royals recalls, "Pete and Re-Pete."

"Those were the days that we didn't even know where

the bars were in Kansas City," Quirk says. "We didn't know the Plaza existed." Every night after home games, the two bachelors would stop off at a neon and gravel spot on Highway 40, the Fun House Pizza. "That was it." Quirk shrugs. "That was the highlight of our year—playing the pinball machines every night and having some pizza."

That was it until they discovered Kansas City's Westport district. The bars. The girls. The nightlife. "Once in a while," Quirk recalls, "maybe once a month, we'd get crazy and go all the way to Westport. It was a younger crowd, and sometimes you could get in without being twenty-one." To say that Brett was dazzled by Westport would be an understatement. To this day, he sometimes breaks his life down into two periods—Before Westport, and After Westport—as if crowded fun-and-laughs bars were his salvation. At the very least, they offered diversion, a rush of excitement. Brett was on the way to his first batting crown, but out in Blue Springs there was no one to talk to about the 3-for-4 nights and the big plays—just the blackest night and the crickets chirping. In Westport he was a celebrity. Strangers approached him freely, just to shake his hand or wish him well. Baseball Annies and star-struck kids haunted the alley outside the Happy Buzzard Tavern, confident of a nightly glimpse of their hero.

The women? "Well . . . I, uh . . . don't want to say I was *horny*," Brett stammers. "I didn't just go out to pick up girls. I just wanted to have a good time. If you got lucky and went home with somebody and you liked them, it was the start of a good relationship. If you didn't like them, hey—" He shrugs. "You just didn't call them anymore."

After Quirk had turned twenty-one too, Westport became almost an every-night affair for the two ball-players. The word got out that Brett was becoming something of a playboy—no mean feat in Kansas City. Rumors circulated that Brett partied till dawn, that he played with a hangover, and that when Nolan Ryan threw fastballs, Brett always swung at the one on the right. "It was just growing up," Brett shrugs. "Everyone goes through it. I'd be in a bar . . . I might have one beer. But people who saw me there stayed maybe two, three hours. They woke up the next day with a hangover and said, 'God, George must feel the same way.'" He laughs. "And some nights I did."

Brett's ability to hoist beers till late the night before with his pal Quirk, and then fall out for extra batting practice in the hot afternoon sun, sweat oozing from every pore, awed his teammates. The line drives spring-ing off his bat, one after the other, when he was admittedly hung over, invited comparisons with the tennis of hustler Bobby Riggs, who played handicapped by galoshes or an empty bucket. But Brett was trying to con no one. Some observers agreed that his partying was just part of growing up. Others suspected that Brett relished the role of the hard-hitting, hard-drinking ballplayer of old. (His big chew of tobacco, cut, at first, with bubble gum, harkened back to the days of the clubhouse spittoon, but Toma, the Royals groundkeeper, had to nag Brett to spit only on the sliding paths—tobacco juice stained the carpet.) Manhood—so important to the youngest of four athletic brothers—came in round, flat tins and pop-top cans.

"There were times I had to talk to him like a father," Whitey Herzog admits. Herzog probably worried that Brett and Quirk would perish some night on the dark, meandering highway back to Blue Springs; and he reminded everyone who listened that an unrelieved diet of alcohol and sex could destroy a ballplayer's career. (Either one in moderation, he added with a wink, was all right.) "I never told George what time to be in bed," Herzog says, "but I told him he had to get his rest."

Brett was not so headstrong that he couldn't see his manager's point of view. Whitey was right! He couldn't go on forever chasing women and drinking till the bars closed, driving 40 miles of dark highway back to the house in Blue Springs. So, to mollify his manager, and to satisfy a few discontents of his own, Brett finally sold his house in Blue Springs and bought a fifty-year-old house in Fairway in the heart of town. Minutes from Westport.

"Before, we were obviously on the wrong side of town for the action," Quirk explains. "The drive home at two in the morning was killing us."

After the 1976 season, Jamie Quirk was traded to the Milwaukee Brewers in a deal that brought catcher Darrell Porter and pitcher Jim Colborn to the Royals. It was one of the best trades general manager Joe Burke ever made, but it broke some hearts in Westport and it left a void in Brett's life. To say that the Morganna affair and similar pranks filled that void is conjecture. In an effort to keep the lights burning at night, Brett wel-

comed visits from his family, and even invited teammates to stay overnight. Westport still counted on his
trade. The quest for good times bordered on decadence,
according to Brett's detractors, who saw in the young
ballplayer a Midwestern version of Broadway Joe
Namath, a love 'em and leave 'em kind of guy who
exploited his celebrity and good looks. His mother saw it
differently. "He was funny," she says, recalling all the
times her son called her in California and said, "Mom,
I'm in love."

"I'd say, 'Oh, how nice, George.'" She laughs knowingly. "The next week he'd call me and say, 'Well, that's
off.' It was a standing joke between us."

The house in Fairway, aside from its convenience for
forays into Westport, was looked on as a renovation
project. "It had a lot of potential," Brett says, "and I
thought it would be a lot of fun to stay home that winter
and redo the whole inside—get a guy, knock out kitchen
cabinets, put in new cabinets, the whole thing." Those
plans were altered somewhat in September 1977 when
Brett, loafing in the bullpen during an afternoon game
with Seattle, heard a terrific crack, looked up, and
watched openmouthed as Clint Hurdle's home run sailed
overhead. Was it fate? Here was yet another rookie—a
refugee, this time, from *Florida*'s beaches—not yet
drinking age, single, and ready to take on the world a
beer at a time.

For six weeks, Hurdle had lived in a Holiday Inn
across the street from the stadium, getting his bearings
and thinking about renting an apartment. Brett finally
stepped forward. According to Hurdle, Brett said, "Hell,

there's no *way* you're gonna pay rent. You come live with me, I'll take care of you." Hurdle laughs. "Little did I know!"

Little did *Brett* know!

"I was the reason George hit .294 that season," Hurdle confesses. The experts attributed Brett's "slump" to injuries, the cynics to alcohol, but Brett blinked his swollen eyelids and moaned to teammates that he was playing with "Hurdle hangover," aggravated by rock 'n' roll malaise. "I've got *loud* tendencies," Hurdle explains, "like the Loud family on *Saturday Night Live*. Even when I whisper, people over there can hear me." Hurdle was the most conspicuous of companions, flamboyant and buoyant of spirit, as loyal and irrepressible as a firehouse dog. "You just wind me up," he laughs, "and once I get going—look *out*! I get louder and louder!" Hurdle's propensity to excess extended to music, where Brett, with his love for country songs, was at a disadvantage. "He had this stereo," Hurdle says, "but he really wouldn't *use* it. George is the type of guy who *has* everything, but he just has it to *have* it. So hell, I'm a rock 'n' roll fanatic!" Hurdle's eyes gleamed. *"Hard* rock. I finally brought my tapes in and started pounding out REO Speedwagon! Mott the Hoople! . . . and George went *berserk*!" Hurdle cackles. *"Foghat!* George says, 'What the hell *is* this? What kinda music *is* this?'"

In a counteroffensive, Brett subjected Hurdle to endless repetitions of Tanya Tucker's "San Antonio Stroll." "George played that song every morning when he got up. *Every* morning. That thing would come out *blasting*." Hurdle rolls his eyes back. "It's like he had this little ritual in the morning. Shower . . . Hair dryer . . . 'San

Antonio Stroll.'" Hurdle beams maliciously. "He'd try to take a nap in the afternoon, then I'd blast him out."

On August 3, the cavalry arrived, pennants flapping, to save Brett: Jamie Quirk was reacquired by the Royals. "I'd heard so much about him," Hurdle recalls. "I felt like I halfway knew the guy. But I think there was a little tension when we first ran into each other, 'cause I was livin' with George, and all I'd heard was *Jamie* and George! *Jamie* and George!" Quirk moved into the house in Fairway—now dubbed Animal House—but if Brett thought Quirk would pacify Hurdle he was mistaken. "It didn't matter to Jamie," Hurdle says.

The neighbors blinked at the increase in traffic. "Our door was always open," Quirk says. "Anybody could wander in, we didn't care who it was. Maybe the outsider looking in saw it as three crazy guys who didn't care about anything, but *we* didn't look at it that way. We were just out to have a good time." The bars closed at one. Then they were off to an after-hours place, or back to Animal House, where carloads of teenagers and eager girls cruised the street. "It was amazing the people that would drop by," Hurdle says. "All *hours*! Just park out in front and stare. Worse than that . . . *inside* the house!" Hurdle's eyebrows shoot up. "There were no locks on any of the bedroom doors! There was no telling when either of those two guys would walk in, just *walk* in. Come in, sit down, turn on the light, *da da da* . . ." Hurdle looks heavenward. "Embarrassing? It got to be *commonplace*! The girls would say, 'Okay, you guys go ahead, play your little game. When you're done, close the door!'" Hurdle groans.

"It really wasn't that wild," Quirk protests. "I don't

consider myself a wild person." He looks a little sheep-
ish. "I guess if I saw a film of myself doing the things I do
. . . I *might* consider myself a wild person." Quirk shows
no reluctance, however, to brand Hurdle. *"Wild,"* he
offers instantly. "Wilder than George and I. *Definitely*
wilder. He was new, he was a rookie, he was the cover
boy, and he just kinda took it all in. He just went wild."
Hurdle's wildness, Quirk contends, was not the diligent
dissipation of the jaded adult, but the gravel-road out-
rageousness of the graduating senior. "It was kinda high
school. Clint was three years younger than us, and he
was still into that rowdy mood. Like in high school, you
might throw something at cars or go around acting like a
football player? George and I were still into fun times,
but nothing rowdy." Quirk's eyes narrow. "Clint was
loud," he sums up. "Clint's *always* been loud. To this
day, he's *still* loud!"

"Jamie was always trying to pull the reins a little bit,"
Hurdle acknowledges cheerfully, cutting into a steak at
a Lee's Summit cafeteria. "He was a stabilizing influence. He cares a little more what people think around
him. He doesn't want to be yelling and shouting, drawin'
a lot of attention. Whereas I don't care!" Hurdle slaps the
table; surrounding diners interrupt their conversations
and stare. "I don't *care,* you know?" He laughs. "Jamie
was always in the middle. You'd have to twist his arm a
little bit to do something. But once the majority vote
came in, he would go along with it. Jamie doesn't like to
cause problems."

The neighbors were surprisingly tolerant. One night,
the three bachelors went partying over in Kansas, all in
the same car—unusual, Hurdle says, because, "You

didn't wanta depend on one of those guys for a ride"—
and Brett found a date and went off with her. Hurdle and
Quirk got back to the house at four in the morning,
drunk, and discovered that they had no key to the front
door. And Brett was not home yet, either. "We said, the
hell with it," Hurdle laughs. "I put my shoes up on the
doorstep and slept on the lawn. A neighbor lady came
out at about six thirty in the morning and asked if we
wanted to come in the house." Hurdle snorts. "There was
dew all over us."

Did such antics constitute a public nuisance? Did the
neighbors complain? Hurdle shakes his head. "Everybody loved George."

And really—despite the Animal House tag, despite the
bachelor habits ("We never had any food in the fridge,"
Hurdle says. "Zero."), and despite the occupants' penchant for dousing each other with ketchup and other
condiments—the Brett household was not quite a frater-
nity house. Brett had hired a maid to do all the
housecleaning, and his decor favored antiques and
framed art. "George has got class," Hurdle says admiringly. "He had an interior decorator!" Hurdle
guffaws. "Telling him what looked good, what didn't look
good."

Jack Brett, too, laughs when asked if his son, as a
youngster, betrayed a discriminating taste. "Well, I
never recognized that." Giving the question serious
thought, he adds, "He might be emulating Ken, 'cause if
you go to Ken's place or Bobby's—they live in side-by-
side condominiums—they're both spotless, absolutely
spotless. And Ken really likes art. He has prints all over
the place, fifty, sixty, seventy years old. George always

stays with Bobby or Ken and he always sees that. He must say, 'Gee whiz, that's pretty nice.'"

George granted that the art in his life functioned as decor, that he was not as passionate about it as Ken was. "Before, I had art posters in my house," he said, "I had cheap art . . . 'cause I wasn't makin' the money." He shrugged. "Now I'm making pretty good money and I have good art." Of course, Brett's quarters had an impersonal look—as if the window display at the Copenhagen Furniture Showroom had been bought and moved in, right down to the last fern and table sculpture. But his bachelor friends certainly didn't mind that. "For a bachelor," Hurdle says, "it was *perfect.*"

Hurdle had but one complaint: George's drinking. Not his *drinking,* actually, but his ability to motivate a baseball the next day with a swollen sun in his eyes and a sober Methodist on the mound. "There's nights you go out," Hurdle says emphatically, "and have your *bad* nights. And then you get a Sunday day game." Hurdle grimaces. "I'd feel like I'd been drug behind a car for about three miles. If I could get *one* hit out of it . . ." Hurdle leans forward and talks in an uncharacteristically hushed voice. "George would go three-for-*three,* three-for-*four,* four-for-*five* . . ." Hurdle straightens and his voice explodes: "Every *time*! It would just tee you off! I'd say to him, 'I'm not goin' out with you anymore! You *embarrass* me!'"

Hurdle grins. "It's the truth."

Brett had signed a five-year contract with the Royals for $1.5 million, so everyone knew he didn't *need* to renovate a house. But it took the winter of 1978-79 for him to reach the same conclusion. "I redid the kitchen and I was beat," he says. "I said, 'Fuck it, I'm selling.'"

"I really liked the house," Jack Brett says. "I stayed with him one weekend there. I said, 'George, you should take ten, or twenty, or thirty thousand dollars and put it into this house and make it everything you want it to be.' But he decided that he didn't want to fix it up. He just saw a house that was better and cost a lot more, and didn't require any fixing up." Just as in 1967, when his big brother's success with baseball and women and the world-at-large had dazzled him, George again measured himself against Kemer. "I was out in California," George remembers, "and my brother was out on the beach. I mean, Kemer had bought a condominium, right on the beach, for a hundred and fifty grand. And I said, 'Son of a *bitch*, I'm making more money than he is and I'm living in this little *dive* place that needs a lot of work! I'm gonna go out and buy a place for the same kind of money!'"

"It was real big," Quirk says, describing Brett's new abode. "It was your typical mansion." Brett's new neighborhood, just off Kansas City's fashionable Ward Parkway, offered a landscape of arching trees, vast lawns, and Georgian houses. Brett and Quirk were still sorethumb bachelors, but now the neighborhood kids drove sports cars instead of minibikes, and wealthy widows walked their dogs in the evening. The Westport crowd now seemed a little young, so Brett and Quirk frequented a new watering hole in the Country Club Plaza, the Granfalloon (which displays in its window a stuffed baby crocodile wearing a cowboy hat). "I didn't get tired of Westport," Brett says, "I think they got tired of me."

In part, he had become wary of the giggly, gushy young women who stalked him in the Westport alley. And he seemed to be groping, consciously, toward a more mature life-style. This pleased manager Herzog, who continued to worry about his star. "George will be forty before he's thirty if he doesn't slow down," Herzog warned. (Predictably, nobody worried about Quirk, a .241 hitter.)

Brett thought he *was* slowing down. His carefree image notwithstanding, he revealed himself now to be a fiscal conservative. He spurned the high-rolling, cut-throat players agents. He carefully plotted his future with trusted advisers from the business community. He entrusted his properties to his millionaire brother Bobby, who invested profitably in southern California real estate. He became an officer—and commercial spokesman—for a Kansas City savings and loan. He drove a Mercedes and lived amidst the surgeons, bankers, and insurance executives.

"I don't spend money," he said at home. He looked around, seeming to take inventory. "The *house* is very expensive. The car is very expensive. But I don't go around and buy things that I don't need." (Hurdle and Quirk might have disagreed—Brett owned some gadgets that he showed little interest in.) Basically, Brett said, his penchant was for houses and land rather than flashy clothes and perishable pleasures. "I'm not tight—by no means am I tight." He gestured at the chrome-framed lithographs of racehorses. "The art you see—it's not cheap art—it's quality stuff." He smiled. "When I was a kid, if I needed a glove, my folks would get it for me. But there were a lot of things I wanted that I didn't get . . . because I didn't need them. I would have loved to have a

TV set in my room, but could I live without it?" He raised his eyebrows questioningly. "That's the way I am now."

To the outsider, Brett's sudden acquisition of a Ward Parkway life-style reeked of status seeking, but his closest friends defended him vigorously. "I knew George when he was making five hundred dollars a month," Jamie Quirk said, "and now he's making millions and millions. And he's exactly the same." John Wathan's wife Nancy agreed completely. "George Brett is one of the most wonderful guys in baseball," she marveled. "He's worth all that money, and the guy doesn't even wear socks!" If George wanted to play with mansions and fancy cars, his friends believed, that's exactly what it was: *play*. There were no signs of stuffiness in his makeup. No amount of camouflage could conceal the man-child playing at life.

"God it was nice," Brett says, recalling that brief interlude in his life. "I really loved it." For one thing, it was quieter; Clint Hurdle had left an atmospheric void by getting married. *"Shocked* us!" Quirk recalls. "We never even knew he had a girlfriend back in Florida."

Actually, Hurdle had dated his future wife, Janet, for some time. But before spring training that year, she had, so to speak, given him his release. "She said, 'I want you to go off and enjoy the big-league experience,'" Hurdle remembers. "I couldn't believe it! I thought, She can't get rid of me!" Thoroughly rattled, Hurdle had kept his feelings for Janet a secret from his teammates during spring training. "I couldn't tell them that *she* dropped *me*," he says. That summer, of course, he had taken Janet's parting words literally—the part about "enjoying the big-league experience." By his own admission, he had crowded a career's worth of frolic into one grueling summer. "Going on the road," he recalls, "I ran into a lot of women." He rolls his eyes up in his head. "Bang, bang, bang, no relationships *whatever*. And I was just burnin' out. Then when I got *benched* . . ." His shoulders fall. "I realized I had nothin' constant. I was either gonna make it and forget about her . . . or come crawlin' back." Hurdle finally decided to crawl. When he had found Janet in Florida, she was with another man, but Hurdle delivered a comic ultimatum. "I said, 'I'm not gonna leave until you marry me.'" Six weeks later, she had. "It's not *can* you live without 'em," Hurdle philosophizes, "it's do you *wanta* live without 'em?" For once, he doesn't laugh. "I wanted her."

Although unnerved by Hurdle's marriage—they expected to hear, next, that Whitey Herzog had joined a Hare Krishna group—both Brett and Quirk later agreed that marriage had had a salutary effect on Hurdle. "It was a good move for Clint," Quirk says. "If he was single right now, who knows? I don't even know if he'd even be in *baseball,* to tell the truth." The taming of Hurdle had also, conveniently, withdrawn a corrupting influence from their own orbits. "If Clint had been single another year," Quirk laughs, "he wouldn't have lived with us, I'll tell you that!"

Brett was changing too, and so was Quirk. Brett had become a celebrity, and the scenario of two handsome bachelors, rattling around in a mansion in the Country Club Plaza district—the playboy fantasy—no longer seemed attainable. Celebrity spoiled it. "The vandalism," Brett explains. "Little kids got a kick out of throwing eggs at my house, toilet-papering it. I think the topper was when they filled my car full of snow." Reluctantly, Brett had put his dream house up for sale. "I decided I needed the privacy."

The move to Quivira Lake had brought Brett full circle: miles from town, a full half hour from Royals Stadium, and alone again—Quirk had decided to take a place of his own on the Plaza. "I was looking at Parkway Towers down in the Plaza," Brett recalls, "and Jesus, that'd be *death,* I think. If I lived down there I could *walk* to those places. I think I'd get tired of it." Brett's after-the-game routine was now reminiscent of his Fun House Pizza days. "I go to the same bar every night," he said, "the Granfalloon, and I have the same thing, a pineapple bacon cheeseburger. Have a couple of beers. And if I'm having a good time, I stay." He shrugged. "If not, I go home."

Private? Cynics suggested that Brett—just turned twenty-seven—was burned out. There was a stricture about burning candles at both ends, and if even *half* the stories about him were true, he had to be down to a pretty short wick.

"Well, he's not as wild as he was in the old days," Quirk admitted. "Now he enjoys his privacy more. And he's taking better care of himself. People thought he'd burn out, but he won't." Others echoed Quirk's belief that Brett's more restrained life-style had contributed to his brilliant baseball seasons of 1979 and 1980. "He disciplined himself more the last year," John Wathan said. "Not going out. Staying ready constantly. He's *gotta* become more private, getting so much recognition,"

"He's matured a lot," Frank White said.

"He's grown up an awful lot this year," Brett's mother added.

They all used different measures of maturity: not showing up for practice with bloodshot eyes, not smashing as many batting helmets, not posing in feathered boas with publicity-hungry strippers. To Brett, life was narrowing down to the essentials. As Bobby Brett put it, "George has really got his program together." Baseball, now, came first—not an obsession, perhaps, but the guiding force in his life. "He keeps it real simple." Still a fatalist, he had at least learned to be a little prudent about his career. When Brett played basketball now, it was not with an assassin's touch. "Last year I used to like to get underneath and"—he hesitated—"not low-bridge . . . but go for rebounds. I'm a little more cautious this year. I'm just like the point guard. I bring the ball up and pass. And when there's a loose ball," he laughed, "I walk the other way." For the first time, he seemed to be dedicating a substantial portion of his energy toward one goal: playing inspired baseball.

Even Brett's attitude toward his accumulating wealth seemed more mature. He seemed somewhat less the kid in the candy store, buying on impulse. He broke his material priorities down to the starkest minimum. He said, "I believe I should have a nice home, a nice car, and I should have a nice bed."

A nice *bed*?

"Well, I spend a lot of time in bed," Brett said. "It's a comfortable bed . . . I spent a lot of money on it . . . you spend a third of your life in bed . . ." He shrugged. "It's just a normal bed, but I *like* it."

*　　*　　*

In the never-ending quest for what is, or is *not* normal, a few enterprising writers have, in the past, tracked down Brett's old girlfriends, plied them with drinks, and asked them intimate questions. As one writer confesses, the results never reach print, but "It's a good way to meet girls." Once, though—in the spring of 1980—Brett's love life spilled into the columns of national tabloids and had local TV news anchors cooing about "wedding bells for George." The occasion was the Miss Universe pageant, and Bob Barker, the ever-grinning emcee, touched off the fireworks by asking Miss New York, Debra Maurice, a seemingly innocent question. "What's your goal in life?" he asked, aiming a microphone at her mouth.

"To marry a baseball player," she replied, provoking laughter from the pageant audience.

Barker seemed bemused. "Anybody in mind?"

"Yes," she said, "George Brett."

Bombs went off in Kansas City (and probably all the other American League cities as well). As the beautiful Miss Maurice offered tidbits about Brett—prodded by Barker—it became obvious that she was talking about a *real* relationship, not a fantasy one. The word "marriage" resounded like a Chinese gong.

"She's great," Brett had said weeks before, in hushed tones. "One of the neatest girls I've ever met. Of course, she's got her life and a busy schedule, and I've got my life and a busy schedule. I don't know if we're going to be able to see each other as much as I'd like to. If we do, it'll be great . . . if not . . ." He had shrugged. Then he had talked about marriage, about his desire to have a family. "I don't wanna get married just to have kids. I wanta have a long relationship with someone. I'm not gonna go out and say, 'Well, I'm twenty-eight, I'm gonna get married and raise some kids.' My brother Ken is thirty-one. He's not married yet, and he's having a hell of a time."

The next afternoon, at Royals Stadium, Brett was not acting like anybody's fiancé. "I dated her," he told a reporter, looking exasperated. "But she didn't have to announce it on television." He was obviously perturbed. (Rumors spread that he had been kept up all night by a ringing phone.) Before long, he was outright angry. Up on the stadium scoreboard, in *lights,* was the announcement that Miss New York, Debra Maurice—George Brett's fiancée—was in attendance and would throw out the ceremonial first pitch. "Oh, my God!" Brett said. "She's here?" The awkward realization came to the press corps in attendance that this was not a Cinderella story at all, but the crash of a relationship.

The Royals beat writers dropped the marriage story as soon as they saw it was sour (although one ghoulish local publisher gleefully reported that Brett had sent Miss Maurice packing on the first Sunday-morning plane to New York). The Miss New York affair did not make Brett look good. His haste to disavow Miss Maurice in the presence of the press and his teammates was unseemly and insensitive. But it was a highly emotional response triggered by one of Brett's greatest fears: that he would fall for a woman whose love for him was part ambition and greed. He was, after all, Kansas City's equivalent to Broadway Joe Namath. Columnist Mike McKenzie, who knows both Brett and Namath, was struck by the similarity. "Joe is immediately a warm guy with a lot of depth and feeling," McKenzie said. "He wants to be a married, family kind of guy. But it's tough for Joe Namath to find a real girl." Celebrity afflicted Brett the same way: the ranks of beautiful, willing young women encouraged a hedonistic life-style, but planted doubts and jealousy in the way of any promising relationship. "If I were a girl, I'd be after Brett's ass, too!" laughed McKenzie (who is married and has two children).

Brett's mother attributed her son's reservations about marriage to his realistic view of baseball life. "Kemmer has influenced him a lot on that," she said. "Ken has always said that he will never get married while he is playing ball. He's seen too much of what goes on." More precisely, Ken had seen the pattern of infidelity that undermines athletes' marriages: the easy women who popped up in hotel bars, the adoring fans behind the dugouts, the brazen pickups who collected at the door of the team bus. Ken put it succinctly: "Guys forget that they're married."

Experience, too, had made Brett wary of commitments. "Whenever he talks about marriage," a friend points out, "he says, 'Hey, I'm a little bit afraid of it.' His parents are divorced, of course." Consequently, although Brett invariably charmed the women (one woman reporter described him as the sort of man parents "wouldn't mind having their daughters bring home to dinner"), he struck some as a cold and chauvinistic man who used women and discarded them. "But he might just find somebody," his mother cautioned, "and all of a sudden, that's it!"

* * *

What Brett didn't deny was his fear that marriage and children might kill a little of the kid in him. "I've always said I liked kids as long as they're not mine," he laughed. "The guys on the team have the greatest kids. Splittorff. Pattin's kids. Patek has the two cutest kids. I like to be around them. They're a lot of fun." But they were not, he observed, *his* kids. "You have to be more dependable, more reliable, with your own kids. When I go out and have dinner sometimes, I like to chew my food and open my mouth—" Brett made a face and went, "Aggh!" He laughed. "I like to stick French fries up my nose. I doubt if I'd do that if the kids were there." He looked thoughtful. "You can't *do* stuff like that."

Brett, of course, was the Royal who was always doing stuff like that—walking through airports wearing large rubber ears, playing third base on his knees, cutting up players' shoes during a game. He reminded one of Gorman Thomas, the Milwaukee Brewers flaky center fielder and slugger who, after a bad game once burned his bat, glove, and uniform in the clubhouse, and observed, "You get a nice blue flame."

"Does Gorman do that stuff?" Brett smiles. "Ernie Harwell had a poem out. 'Boys of Summer.' It sent chills up my spine. The final line is, 'We're just a bunch of grown men playing a little boys game.'" Brett shook his head. "You see guys like Marty Pattin, who's thirty-three, thirty-four . . . the stuff he does sometimes is something that a twelve-year-old boy would do—" Talking like a duck, for instance? Brett nodded. "And it's *fun.*"

The hazard, then, as Brett saw it, was not one of burning out early—but of growing up too soon. "I'd hate to live to be sixty years old," he says, "then die, and not have had a good time."

"He still does some silly things," Jack Brett says. "He does things without thinking. For instance, I've never backed a car out of a garage and taken the door off it because I forgot the door was closed . . . He's *done* that." Jack heaves a sigh and smiles. "I think the big kid is still there."

2. The Pitch

"Gotta get ready for the *Goose,*" Clint Hurdle said.

A pitch floated up to the batting cage and Hurdle took an enormous whiplash cut, grunting so loud—whooping, almost, from the bottom of his diaphragm—*"Hunnnh!"*—that a coach hitting ground balls to the infield turned in bewilderment. "I just read this book about physical *exertion,*" Hurdle grinned, kicking baseballs out from under his feet and poking at them with the end of his bat. "The idea is that during physical exertion, you've gotta make *noise!* That's how you get *power!* You see? I'm at a disadvantage against the Goose. He *grunts* when he throws, but I don't grunt when I swing." Hurdle assumed his stance, eyed the pitch, and swung with another explosive grunt, a resounding *"Hunnnh!"* The result was a topped grounder which rolled to a stop near the mound. "I'm trying it out," he said. *"Hunnnh!"* This ball struck the top of the cage and almost rebounded into his face. "But it's too hard concentrating on grunting!" He looked back through the cage at his snickering teammates, a self-satisfied grin on his face. "You know?" He turned back to the mound, squinting craftily, imagining that the batting practice pitcher was Goose Gossage, the hulking, fastballing bullpen star of the Yankees. "Grunt when you throw!" he yelled out to the mound. He waggled his bat and lowered his voice to a relative murmur. "If you ain't hit it by the time you hear the grunt—" He swung, *"Hunnh!"* and lined the ball into right field.

Hurdle grinned. "—you're *gone."*

The Goose.

Every year there was a pitcher that American League hitters regarded with awe, joked about, nervously praised. For some seasons it had been Nolan Ryan, the California Angels dangerously fast, dangerously wild hurler whose best-pitch, a 102 MPH fastball, was referred to as the "death ball" or "the widow-maker." In 1980, the pitcher was Richard Michael Gossage. Five times an All-Star. Four times a twenty-five-plus-saves reliever. Tied with the Royals Dan Quisenberry for the league lead in saves with thirty-three. A 6-foot-3, 217-pound exterminator with one pitch—a total-effort, 100 MPH fastball—issued without deliberation or delay, *bam-bam-bam,* like a sociopathic prizefighter pummeling a patsy. "Guys like him—they look like they're right on top of you," said U. L. Washington. "He's about six-six or six-seven, maybe two hundred and thirty pounds"—

Washington tongued the trademark toothpick in his mouth, unaware that he had overestimated Gossage's stature—"and when he's throwin' that hard . . . you've gotta feel that he's *cheatin'*." Time after time, the brutally efficient Gossage had dispatched opponents in the late innings of important ball games, throwing nothing but "heat" in a kind of angry haste that made hitters edgy and tentative. "There's only one thing that keeps us from beating the Yankees," Whitey Herzog had said the year before, "and that's Gossage."

Few of the Royals "prepared" for the Goose, as did Hurdle, on the eve of the 1980 American League Championship Series. They talked, instead, of the necessity of "getting the jump," taking the early lead in a game and holding on. The Royals had won eight out of twelve games from New York in 1980, but nothing could have flattered the Yankees more than this admission that they were almost *conceded* victory if they led or were tied in the seventh inning or later. "We're not afraid of Gossage," Hal McRae reflected soberly. "We'd just rather hit against some of their other guys."

Game after game, night after night, in the fluorescent twilight of the tunnel, McRae was preparing for the play-offs, if not for Gossage. "I've come up with a different routine," he said. "The running is gonna continue, but I jump a lot of rope now. It gets my blood flowing and I get a sweat." The bizarre picture flashed in one's mind of George Brett, back in the dark tunnel, savagely smashing a shopping cart with a baseball bat, while McRae hopped up and down the runway, huffing and puffing, skipping rope. "The last half of the season I did this every day," McRae continued, "and I hit real well. I really got the adrenaline going." The best part of the routine, he added, was that it provided him a precious feeling. "I get the feeling," he said, "that I'm playing the outfield on a Sunday afternoon and it's a hundred and two degrees."

In 1980, his shoulder finally healing, McRae had hit .297 with 83 runs batted in. One night, against the Texas Rangers, McRae had driven two balls over the distant center-field wall in Royals Stadium and had had two more balls caught off that same wall. "I surprised myself," he said. "One morning I woke up and I just had that feeling: 'You can still do it. You can do it almost as good as you used to do it.'"

The rejuvenation of Hal McRae buoyed the Royals, but his was not the only revival show on the Royals in 1980. "I'm waking up," Clint Hurdle announced. The born-again ballplayer had returned to the majors as a left-handed platooner in right field, batting .294 with 10 homers and 60 RBIs. His performance quieted those in the right-field bleachers who in April had booed his every move in anger over the trade that had sent bleacher favorite Al Cowens to California for first baseman Willie Aikens. "I took a beating, there's no doubt," Hurdle said good-naturedly. "The low point of my career was last year in Omaha. I was a better ballplayer at nineteen than I was at twenty-one!" Hurdle grimaced. "But I *needed* to get shot down a little bit. Find my values. If things had worked out, I'd be a monster. My ego would probably be as big as this *room!*" There were those who said that Hurdle's ego *was* that size, but he claimed that his love of "hotdogging," to which he confessed—he wore six-inch wristbands—did not mean he was big-headed. "You're trying to hide that you're scared," he said, remembering the frustration of his first two major league seasons. "You build up an air that says, 'Nothing bothers me.' Your security is through your mouth." Another positive step, he said slyly, was his decision to limit his contact with known incorrigibles like George Brett and Jamie Quirk. "I turned left from those guys two years ago," he laughed. "Got married, cleaned up my act, taking a shower at least once a week now and everything! Those guys could be eternal bachelors. They can handle it." He shrugged, grinning. "I couldn't."

The genuine resurrection on the Royals was the reappearance of Ken Brett in a major league uniform. He had spent the better part of 1980 browning himself on the warm sands outside his Hermosa Beach condominium until the Royals signed him on August 18. "I thought it was over," he admitted, reflecting on his springtime release from the Los Angeles Dodgers. "I hurt my arm pretty bad on March twelfth—and on March twenty-sixth they released me." The hammer had fallen fast and heavy, he thought, considering his 30 relief appearances, 4-3 record, and 3.45 ERA for the Dodgers in 1979. "I know this is a business," he said. "Still, you can show compassion, and I thought they'd done it the wrong way. If your gonna tell a girl you don't love her, you don't tell her, 'Get out of my life.'"

Ken had faced the future realistically. "My arm was

legitimately injured. It was hanging on. And I was tired of knocking on people's doors. So I laid on the beach all summer, not doing anything, baseball-wise. I jogged. But I didn't *look* at a box score. Didn't want to." With rest, his elbow healed; and when the Royals, starved for left-handed pitching, made their offer, Kemer accepted. He pitched in a minor league uniform for the first time in over ten years, and it was like a repeat of his rookie season with the Red Sox. He was brought up by the Royals for a late-season look, pitched thirteen innings without surrendering a run, and was kept on the roster for the play-offs—and a possible second World Series.

Skeptics—and those unfamiliar with the Royals bullpen depth—joked that Ken Brett had been purchased to keep his celebrity brother company, but George scoffed at that idea. "Kemer? I hardly ever see him. He spends more time with Jamie than he does with me. After a game I ask them what they're doing. They say, 'Oh, we're going out, see you later! They want me to go home and get my rest. Some friends!"

"It's very, very difficult to go out with George anymore," Quirk explained. "First of all, you almost feel like you're left out of everything, 'cause people are there to see George Brett. Sometimes I feel like I'm sort of the hang-around guy. So when Ken joined the club, *Ken* and I started to go out a bit. And it wasn't because we didn't want to go out with George, but George was a .400 hitter with a thirty-game hitting streak and it was *impossible*. So we just left him alone. Which was bad, but it was the only way it could be done." Quirk smiled. "George has gone back to the Fun House Pizza type of place. He'd rather go there, drink a beer, eat a pizza, and go home. Me, I don't get bothered like that. I can still go to the bars. It's nothing like the mob scene when George comes in."

Ken Brett was more than a surrogate George for Quirk; he was also a surrogate Quirk for the press, who had long looked to George's "buddy" for insight into the Brett temperament. "Jamie does more interviews than a lot of the guys on the team that play every day," John Wathan sympathized. "We kid him about it all the time. When there's a writer sitting next to him, we know what they're asking. They aren't talking about Jamie Quirk. They're talking about *George*. It isn't easy for him. To be asked, day in and day out, questions about somebody else, not yourself, is tough." Now, Ken Brett drew the writers looking for a fresh angle. Sometimes he disappointed them with his honesty. "I never saw him grow up," Ken confessed. "My father *said* George was going to be the best in the family, and he's become the best in *baseball*." Ken put on an ironic grin. "My father was right."

Ken had long since resigned himself to being known as George Brett's older brother, and his sense of irony was developed enough to appreciate the switch in roles. But Quirk had not enjoyed the flirtation with fame that Ken Brett had, not since turning down a Notre Dame football scholarship to sign with the Royals as a number one draft choice in 1972. "It's hurt Jamie," Charley Lau said. "There was a period when Jamie was the bright young prospect and maybe George was *not*. All of a sudden, George came to the front and Jamie floundered a little bit, due to a little lack of ability—not desire. But Jamie's a superb young man and he handled it well. I don't think you can find a better twosome. They drank together, ate together, lived together, and are just as compatible as two people can be."

The stability of Brett's male relationships—his "buddies," as one writer put it—was in marked contrast to the fleeting quality of his romances. "People don't realize George and I have been friends for ten years," Quirk said one afternoon in the Royals offices. "They started kidding around, saying I was riding on his coattails, things like that. That annoyed me. But George never said anything like that. Just people looking from the outside in. To this day—MVP, superstar that he is—we've still got that same friendship we had when I was seventeen and he was eighteen."

Charley Lau echoed Quirk. "We're as close as we ever were," the Yankee coach said. "There's just a very warm feeling between us that will never go away regardless of who I work for and who George plays for."

A gleam came to Lau's eye. "But hey, I'm a Yankee and I want to win. That's the only way that I'll be paid. If we lose, I'll be fired." (Lau, apparently, had fathomed the George Steinbrenner temperament.) "As much as I like George Brett, I will do everything in my power to get him out."

It would have taken a lasso in 1980. In ten games Brett had savaged the Yankees for a .425 batting average with 3 doubles, 2 triples, 4 home runs, and 22

RBIs. So effective was Brett at Yankee Stadium that speed merchant Willie Wilson would not steal second base whenever Brett was at the plate. "I wouldn't steal because George was pulling the ball," Wilson said, "aiming for that short-right-field porch." By staying at first, Wilson froze the first baseman on the bag, leaving Brett a huge gap on the right side of the infield. Lau muttered that his Frankenstein Monster had turned on him.

Fortunately for Lau, the Jacob's ladders in his laboratory still sparked, and the Yankee peasantry—the fans, that is—were not at his castle gates with burning fagots. They had their own monster, one with a candy bar named after him. Reggie Jackson, under Lau's tutelage, had surprised everyone in 1980 by hitting .300 for the first time in his lengthy career—and with no loss of power, smashing 41 home runs and driving in 111. "Reggie and I talked in years previous," Lau reflected, "back in Oakland. And it didn't work out between us. . . . I think through my stupidity. So with my going to the Yankees, there were a lot of people just sitting back and saying, 'Well, he might have had some success in Kansas City with Punch and Judys—but let's see what happens when he mingles with the big boys!" Lau's voice was hoarse. "So Reggie—Reggie's at an age, what, thirty-five? thirty-six?" Lau pondered the implications of baseball senility. "And probably the most famous name in baseball. But he came to me. He said, 'Talk. Let's go to work.'" The words echoed those of Hal McRae, seven years before—a roll-up-the-sleeves, let's-do-it declaration that belied Jackson's image as a stubborn egomaniac. "Reggie doesn't believe in a lot of things," Lau admitted, "but if he believes in *one* thing it'll work for him." Lau had not changed Jackson's swing—Reggie still corkscrewed to his knees in a violent effort to send balls into orbit—but Lau got him to go to left field more often, to hit the ball hard in all directions, to achieve a consistency lacking in his early career. "I just think he has a more commonsense approach to mechanics right now," Lau said. "Whether it was me, or whether he's just maturing like wine, whatever . . ." He shrugged. "I'm as close to a lot of the Yankees now as I was to the Kansas City players. If you have answers—people will listen."

The *Kansas City Times*'s Mike McKenzie had listened to Lau one afternoon on the Yankees last road trip to Kansas City, but he hadn't believed his ears. "Never interviewed the man," McKenzie prefaced with a big smile. "Never met him!"

McKenzie had been standing in the Yankee dugout, waiting to interview Goose Gossage, when Lau had walked over from the batting cage. "Lau stands at the top of the dugout and points to me and says, 'Mike McKenzie, right?' I stood up and extended my hand and said, 'Yeah, Charley . . .' and before I could get any farther he put his finger in my face, he's trembling, and he says, 'I think you're a low-down sonofabitch!'"

McKenzie looked bewildered. "I said, 'What's this about?'

"Lau said, 'I just wanted you to hear it straight from me that I think you're a low-down sonofabitch.'

"I said, 'Charley, you don't know me and I don't know you. You wanta talk this out?'

"He says, 'I don't even want to talk to you. *Ever.*' And he walks away!"

McKenzie laughed. "I'd never met Charley Lau, I didn't know any of his friends, never interviewed him. I'd only written about him casually. So I asked around. It seems I had done a story with Hurdle in the winter, on the phone from Venezuela. And Hurdle was the only guy you could find on the Royals who was anti Lau. He thought he'd ruined him. Apparently, somebody'd clipped that out of the newspaper and mailed it to Charley. And I guess for seven months he had had that simmering inside him."

Clint Hurdle seemed embarrassed about the McKenzie-Lau run-in. "I guess Mike just hit him at a bad time," Hurdle said. "Charley doesn't show much emotion, but when he gets mad"—Hurdle's voice dropped conspiratorially—"he gets *mad!*" Hurdle sighed. "Charley and I have talked. I was mad, I was young. I couldn't understand being in the big leagues and having one guy wanting you to do it one way, and the other guy wanting you to do it the other way. And neither one of them is gonna give! People were running to me saying, 'You got Lau fired!'" He shrugged helplessly. "I tried to evade the issue, but a couple of articles came out where he got popped pretty good for my failure. Which I never said! I'm not that vain to say it's *his* fault I didn't hit." Hurdle shook his head sadly. "I feel bad about it now, 'cause I really didn't understand the situation. Charley puts a lot of stock in a relationship. I know he did with me. I'd love to work with him again now that I've grown up a little bit. Learn a little bit more about the game. Even about him." Hurdle's voice was emphatic: "He's the *best.*"

*　　*　　*

On the family front, Ethel Johnson read a newspaper headline that made her moan: THE BATTLING BRETT BROTHERS. The article resurrected the six-year-old Thanksgiving Eve battle between John and George, and left the impression that the Brett parents dismissed street fighting among adults as "high-spirited" fooling around. "Ohhh, I didn't like it at all," she chuckled. "Some of it had truth to it, but other parts didn't." Had her boys been as difficult to raise as the article implied? "Oh, no," she scoffed. "They were a handful, but they helped around. They worked, they all had their chores to do. They all had to clean up their bedrooms, make their beds and things before I got home from work." The fighting? "I think it was exaggerated."

Jack Brett, while admitting to his sons' occasional obstreperousness, suggested that their fraternal competitiveness now found milder outlets. "They still enjoy needling each other and doing things to each other," he said. "One of the most popular things they do to each other now is stick each other with the bill. They really enjoy it—it's developed into an art. They'll buy clothes and tell the store, 'Send the bill to John' or 'Send the bill to Bobby.' John was in Kansas City with some people and went to the Stadium Club, and I guess they had lobster dinners. John signed the check to George Brett and he wrote, 'Thanks, Lou.'"

Perhaps to protect his dwindling fortune, George was talking about moving. This time to a ranch, his father said, somewhere in open country. "I just asked him how big, and he said, 'Oh, forty acres.'" Jack laughed. "George's experience with ranching, though, is that he visits John's friend Mike Battle, who owns a ranch in

Texas. Mike has one hundred or two hundred or three hundred or six hundred acres in Texas. George goes down there for a week and they go hunting. George doesn't see the day-to-day work that's entailed in running a ranch. So we're all saying, 'George, who's going to run it for you?' And he says, 'I'll hire somebody,' And we say, *'George'*—Jack Brett's voice drops to a patronizing murmur—"'you gotta run it yourself.'"

It was apparent that Jack Brett still questioned his youngest son's maturity, and could not resist the impulse to question every decision he made. But George no longer reacted to the paternal oversight by smashing mirrors or ripping the phones out of hotel-room walls. And Jack Brett no longer questioned his son's playing skills. ("It's hard for my dad," Bobby Brett laughed, "to say, 'Goddamn, you shoulda hit .400!'") Gradually, George's love of family had begun to overcome his sense of frustration and rage. "There's a part of him, I think, that still hates his dad," Hurdle mused, "but George isn't the type to really hold a grudge, and I really think he can see things now from a father's standpoint. I think they've probably pulled together from that aspect. His dad realizes he might have made some mistakes, not been as close as he should. Jack's probably kicking himself in the butt for everything that went on at home. And now, to see his son do all this. . . ." Hurdle shook his head. "He's probably enjoying it, but can you imagine how much *more* he'd be enjoying it? How much prouder he could be?"

The first two games of the 1980 American League Championship Series were played in Kansas City. As they had hoped, the Royals led both games in the late innings and never had to face Goose Gossage. Larry Gura won the first game, 7-2, supported by Willie Aikens' two-run single in the third. Brett's home run in the seventh inning, his fifth in ALCS play, tied him with Reggie Jackson and Sal Bando for the all-time lead. The next day, Dennis Leonard and Dan Quisenberry combined for a 3-2 win, the Yankees tying run, represented by Willie Randolph, dying in the eighth, gunned down at the plate by a relay throw from Brett to Darrell Porter.

Kansas City fans were not overconfident. The anticipation of triumph had cost them spiritually many times in play-offs with the Yankees, and they dared not hope too hard, lest the spell be shattered. The Royals traveled to New York needing only one victory in three games to win their first pennant ever, but some observers feared that the least setback—say, a third-game loss—would turn the tide in favor of the Yankees. On the eve of the third game, Kansas City TV stations ran interviews with still-cocky Yankee fans, and showed kids in Yankee helmets with their hands around their own throats, their eyes bugged out, tongues protruding—prophesies of a Royals choke. "We can win three under any circumstances," Yankee manager Dick Howser had told a press throng after the loss in game two. "This just makes it a little tougher. We'll be ready when we get home."

The third game was played at Yankee Stadium on a Saturday night, October 11, and a gloomy, drizzly night it was. Tommy John and Paul Splittorff exchanged scoreless innings through three, but rain began falling in the top of the fourth, causing umbrellas to sprout in the stands. The tarp was rolled out and the game delayed for thirty-two minutes, while players on both benches huddled in their warm-up jackets, looking morose, arms folded, eyes uplifted. The rain soon dwindled to a mist, and when the tense battle resumed, Frank White stung John for a line-drive homer to left in the fifth inning, giving the Royals a 1-0 advantage— "Gossage insurance," they called it. But the Yankees scored two in the sixth, and the Royals' fears were realized: they trailed the Yankees in Yankee Stadium in the last third of the game, with Tommy John on the mound and Goose Gossage in the bullpen. "If we got far enough ahead," U. L. Washington recalls, "we knew we weren't gonna see him." But now the slightest lapse by John, even an accident, a bad break, an error—and Goose would take the mound with his upper-nineties fastball (which, compared to John's junky sinker, would burn the plate like a laser).

It happened in the Royals seventh. With two outs, Willie Wilson doubled, and before the speedy outfielder had even tagged second, everybody knew: John was gone. The crowd roared as Gossage came in from the bullpen; they roared as he prepared to pitch to Washington; and it was only the dangerous livers among them who hoped that Washington would somehow get aboard to set up a classic duel with the batter in the on-deck circle: George Brett. The Royals contingent, of course, could think of nothing else. "A lot of times this year, I got the 'semibig' hit," Washington laughed later. "Everyone was calling me that: 'semibig hit.' In four or five games I got the hit that prolonged an inning where George could win the game for us. But I'd faced Gossage ten or twelve times and he'd really dominated me. I'd never gotten a hit off him."

Still, if somehow—if somehow Washington could avoid being blown away—it would come down to Brett versus Gossage in the court of last appeals. "There's no doubt in my mind that George is the best situation hitter in baseball," Fred White says. "If you need a double in the ninth inning, a triple in the ninth, or a home run, he's probably the best guy to get you what you need." But then, you could say the same for the Goose: if you needed the strikeout in the ninth, if you needed to deal with the enemy slugger with the bags filled, the Yankees knew that the *Goose* gave you exactly what you needed. There it was. Irresistible force meets immovable object. Power meets power. Rock meets hard place.

And only U. L. Washington stood in the way. . . .

In the first inning of George Brett's first play-off game against the Yankees—October 9, 1976, at Royals Stadium—he fielded a ground ball, cocked his arm, and fired a strong throw about a foot above the glove of a leaping John Mayberry for an error. A minute later, with the bases loaded, Brett fielded another grounder, stepped on third for the force-out, and uncorked a *low* throw that skipped past Mayberry for another error. Two runs scored.

In the bottom of the fourth inning, the Yankee manager, Billy Martin—his sympathies stirred by Brett's misfortune—yelled something consoling to the Royals third baseman when he came to the plate. "Your brother's a cocksucker!" he shouted. "Your brother's a cocksucker!" Brett stared into the Yankee dugout, shocked. Then he stepped into the box and rifled a Catfish Hunter pitch into right field for a single. In the seventh inning, Martin yelled, "Your brother's a cocksucker!" and Brett ripped another single. In the ninth, Brett singled hard again. "Your brother's a cocksucker!" Martin yelled.

"Every time I came to bat," a dejected Brett said, sitting in the clubhouse after the Royals had fallen, 4-1. "That's really high-class, really a tribute to baseball." Martin's remarks had been rooted in an early-season trade. The Yankees had shipped Ken Brett to the White Sox two days after Martin had assured the left-hander he wouldn't be traded, and Martin—a master of psychological abuse—had jumped at the family angle to get at brother George. ("Personally, I like the guy," Martin said later. "He's a great player.") In the Royals clubhouse, Brett was asked if he now wanted to beat the Yankees especially badly because of their treatment of his brother. "If I had a grudge against every team that traded my brother," he replied, "I'd have a grudge against every team in baseball."

Nevertheless, from that day forward he played the Yankees as if he did hold a grudge. Some of the enduring memories of championship series play belonged to George Brett, starting with his stirring three-run homer to tie the Yankees at 6-6 in the eighth inning of the final game of the 1976 series—a shocking blow that hushed a jubilant Yankee Stadium crowd (until Chris Chambliss restored bedlam in the ninth with his pennant-winning solo shot off Royals reliever Mark Littell). A year later, in an even more bitter Royals failure, the play that set the tone of the deciding game—if not the outcome—was Brett's first-inning triple, which ended in a fist-swinging scuffle at third with Yankee third baseman Graig Nettles. And finally, the memorable afternoon in Yankee Stadium in the third game of the 1978 series, when Brett blasted three consecutive homers off Catfish Hunter— only to be answered in the eighth inning by a game-winning, two-run Thurman Munson shot to deep left center off Doug Bird. "We always lost!" Brett laughed later. His greatest moments seemed always to be swallowed up in Royal frustration. Fans remembers his red-eyed grief in the clubhouse after Chambliss' spoiling homer, or his disgusted, arms-folded posture when Munson lumbered around third after his 1978 home run, looking, as one observer put it, "like a newspaper truck with a poster on the side reading ROYALS LOSE AGAIN!"

"That would have been the greatest thing in my life, to win one of those series," Brett said, looking back. From time to time he would sit in front of the Betamax in his game room and play back the home runs against Hunter, savoring the moments of glory in Yankee Stadium—so poignant in light of his father's old dream that Ken Brett might one day replace Mickey Mantle as center fielder of the Yankees. Notwithstanding his allegiance to Charley Lau's theories, the kid in George Brett still reveled in the clutch home run. He enjoyed his reputation as a hitter who could, in Bill Veeck's words, "go for the downs" when the game was on the line. "I think there's some pitchers you can do it against," Brett admitted. "You can't do it against a Ron Guidry or a Tommy John, but it's a little easier for me off of right-handed pitchers. But no matter how much I know a pitcher"—he seemed to be hearing Charley Lau's voice, like a conscience—"I still don't guess. I just try to see the ball and react."

The key to success under pressure, Brett believed, lay in one's ability to relax, to maintain one's concentration. "Charley used to tell me, 'Just relax and take a good fluid swing.'" Brett remembered a program the Royals had sponsored in 1972, formulated by Dr. Bill Harrison, a California eye doctor who was interested in techniques of concentration, relaxation, "success-imaging," and "centering." "We did things like spell words backwards while jumping on a trampoline, doing jumping jacks with a strobe light on, and so on. You'd be trying so *hard* to do that that you wouldn't be able to do that. He'd say, 'Don't try hard, try *easier*. It relaxes your mind, it relaxes your body.' A lot of guys, when the crowd starts cheering they get tense. They want to hit the ball in the water fountain in Kansas City, they want to hit the ball off the scoreboard. They try so *hard*. I just try *easier*. And let my natural ability do it."

In 1978, a competing philosophy had its headquarters several stalls away from Brett's in the Royals clubhouse. A large ceramic vulture—a glowering cousin of the Maltese Falcon, potbellied, with crooked orange neck and malevolent yellow beak—perched above the locker. The inscription read: ROYALS BULLPEN VULTURE. In front of the stall, in a director's chair, sat a man in a Royals uniform whose every move, even the tying of a shoelace, seemed a little too quick, a shade too tight, as if the task were too small for the available energy. The name on the stall was Al Hrabosky.

"I used to have a very uncontrollable temper," the man said. He ran his fingers through his luxurious shock of black hair and sat impassively for a moment. The Fu Manchu mustache evoked cinema associations of Oriental violence rather than genuine depravity, but the piercing gaze betrayed a legitimate glimpse of the notorious "Mad Hungarian," whose menacing fastball and Rasputinlike powers on the mound had earned a niche in modern baseball lore.

"Once I got mad," Hrabosky continued, calmly rolling the white baseball socks down over the tops of his blue stirrups, "I was totally useless. I would feel a surge of power going through my body from the increased adrenaline, but I lost total concentration. All my manager could do was yank me out, 'cause I was useless."

Enter the Mad Hungarian. "When I started walking off the back of the mound," Hrabosky said, "I was at a stage where I was destined to go back to the minors. So I started walking off the back of the mound purely for concentration." That moment of meditation, that self-induced trancelike state, had bestowed a surprising advantage: it had allowed Hrabosky to transfer his fatal flaw, his anger, into a unique asset. "I tried to capture that adrenaline and channel it against the hitter. Then I tried to go one more step and use this anger in what I call a 'controlled hate mood.'" Hrabosky whipped himself into a frenzy before he ever threw a pitch. His back to the batter, the Mad Hungarian hunched his shoulders, lowered his head, and squeezed the ball savagely in his bare hands, lingering over past violations of his dignity: base hits, embarrassing walks, home runs, anything warranting revenge. If baseball memories did not suffice, he grasped at less obvious grievances: "I don't like the town," Hrabosky said gravely. "Somebody looked at me wrong that day." He smiled. "Anything in the world to make me want to hate." The glove would go back on the hand; there was a sudden suspension of motion, an instant of deliberate murderous contemplation, and finally the Hungarian would slam fist and ball into the glove and wheel angrily toward the mound, glaring at the batter, who waited to deflect Hrabosky's missiles with a usually inadequate stick. "I try to make it a one-on-one battle." Hrabosky said. "I *defy* him to stand in the batter's box. If I had another foot in size or weighed another fifty pounds, I could intimidate through size. But I don't have that, so I try to do it with my competitive spirit—this guy who stomps around and acts crazy out there. I really try to make a guy think, Hey, this guy's *crazy*. I've got a wife and two kids at home and this guy might hit me in the head, he might maim me. . . .

"That's my kingdom out there," Hrabosky said with a grand gesture. "That's my throne on the mound and nobody violates it." But he added, "What I do on the mound—it's a time bomb. If you're successful, the people tolerate it, they like it"—he shrugged—"they *dis*like it. But when you fail, you're the spectacle of the world."

George Brett's response to Hrabosky's "kingdom of rage"? "I say *don't* key up," he said. *"Don't* psych yourself up." The time-bomb metaphor fit Brett's temperament as well as Hrabosky's madman act, but an explosion of anger at the plate, Brett believed, would render him helpless against a pitcher. Brett expelled his demons in the dugout or the clubhouse by kicking helmets and grocery carts, by scattering bats, by ranting and cursing until suddenly the anger was gone, the mind was clear, and the tension had fled his muscles. "George has never been accused of overthinking a situation," Royals director of player personnel John Schuerholz says. "He's never been too profound about the game."

"Most players overthink," Bobby Brett agrees, "but George keeps it real simple. It's like he's a robot up there. He's got his hitting programmed."

George Brett laughed. "Hungo says, 'Psych up!' That's how he signs his autographs—'To Johnny—psych up!' But when you get too psyched up, the tension is too great. So I'll write on the other side of the ball—"

George grinned. "—'To Johnny—psych *down.*'"

If I had another foot in size or weighed another fifty pounds, I could intimidate through size.

Al Hrabosky could have said, "If I were Goose Gossage . . ."

U. L. Washington, a switch-hitter, stepped in as a left-handed hitter against the Goose—a stride or two closer to first base—and all but bought a ticket. "The first five pitches, I took," Washington said afterward. "I was just trying to let George get up to bat." Gossage went to two balls and no strikes on Washington, but then came back to a full count against the toothpick-gnawing voyeur at the plate. *I gotta put some wood on it now,* Washington told himself, but he didn't have to tell himself what pitch to expect. "You know Gossage. When he gets out there he's just gonna throw gas." The payoff pitch was an inside fastball—too close to take—and Washington swung in desperation—"I got just enough wood on it to get it over his head"—chopping a puny grounder that bounced over Gossage and dribbled along the grass to the left of second base—"and as soon as I saw where the ball was hit—"

Washington smiled and digressed. "I used to have a bad habit earlier in the year of watching the ball," he said. "But I made up my mind the last part of the year to see where it was heading, and then put my head down and *hustle* on down to first. And it paid off this time. I took one glance at the ball and saw Willie Randolph had a chance at it, but he was gonna have to get to it and throw off-balance with something on it to get me."

Randolph *did* get to it, *did* throw off-balance, but he couldn't get enough on the throw to catch Washington, whose last lunging stride to the bag was a split-second ahead of the slap of ball on leather. ("Earlier in the year, I'd have been thrown out," Washington said.) A cresting roar from the stands disintegrated into a confused murmur, a growing commotion. Two on. Two out. And *George Brett* coming to the plate.

Bruce Carnahan, the Royals publications director, remembers the moment. "I was sitting in the Yankee press box. As soon as U.L. got on base, almost all eyes met, *knowing* that something was going to happen." Royals broadcaster Fred White had the same feeling. "Probably thousands of people will tell you now they expected George to do what he did. But I honestly *did,* on the air. I told myself when George came up, Be ready, but don't make a mistake."

The Yankee faithful, over 56,000 strong, roared in anticipation as Brett stood outside the batter's box. He took a deep breath, refusing to look out at the mound, where Gossage waited, ball in hand, foot on the rubber, a ponderous, anxious presence. Then Brett stepped into the box, moving dirt around with his spikes, digging in . . . and only *then* faced the Goose, rhythmically working his bat through the strike zone, settling his weight on his back foot.

"Everything was at a fever pitch," Carnahan remembers. "And then *bang,* they were stunned."

The first pitch? Who expected the first pitch? Brett unwound on Gossage's 98-mile-an-hour fastball and a blur of white shot up into the lights. "It was a crack of the bat," recalls John Wathan, "that just resounded in the whole ballpark. You knew immediately, even from our poor angle in the third-base dugout, that it was gone. George just crushed it. The only thing we were concerned about at first was that it might hook foul. But when we saw that it was upper deck—that put the icing on the cake."

"I thought it had a chance to go to Coney *Island* when he hit it," said John Schuerholz. "It was one of the most awesome shots in a critical situation I've ever seen."

"I didn't know if it was a pop-up or what," U. L. Washington laughed later. "I couldn't really tell 'cause the ball was hit right over my head at first. But I looked out and I watched Reggie and he just looked disgusted. I started jumpin'. And the ball landed up in the upper deck! I don't know how I thought it had a chance to be caught—just the angle, I guess. I couldn't believe it! I jumped all the way around the bases."

For a few seconds after the ball disappeared into the third tier, the sounds were eerily like those of panic at a fire—mingled shouting and screaming. Then a sepulchral gloom coursed through the stands—not total silence, as many remember, but a dispirited, hushed atmosphere composed of scattered murmuring and an occasional isolated yelp by a Royals fan and high-pitched screams by frustrated Yankee partisans. It was a sound—a climate really—remembered from Royals Stadium after the final out of the fifth game of the 1977 series, when the pennant had slipped away from the Royals in a catastrophic ninth inning. The hushed spectators had stood at their seats in the chill night air, going nowhere, staring around and blinking and avoiding each other's eyes. (Fred Patek, the Royals shortstop, said at the time, "It was like somebody really *died.")* Now it was the Yankees' turn. Wilson scored. Washington scored. George Brett bounded across home plate with the fourth run. "It was like the Ali-Frazier fight," Bruce Carnahan said, "when Ali knocked him out in the first round. There's a lot of Yankee fans that will never forget George Brett's home run off Goose Gossage."

Nor would Royals fans. "At that point we knew we had it," John Wathan says. "We *knew* we were finally gonna be in the World Series."

In the clubhouse afterward, with champagne splashing and towels flying and players whooping ridiculously, Royals pitcher Dennis Leonard summed it up in words he must have written in some honky-tonk: "It's nice to be in the clubhouse where the champagne is flowing rather than in the clubhouse where the beer and the teardrops are falling." Jim Frey, going to the World Series in his rookie year as a manager, grinned broadly. "The Goose was the guy they said was gonna shoot us down. And George nailed him."

Reliever Dan Quisenberry had staved off late-inning

disaster—the Yankees had loaded the bases in the eighth with none out, only to have their rally fizzle flukily when Rick Cerone's hard liner to U. L. Washington was turned into a double play. Frank White had been voted the Most Valuable Player for his standout fielding and hitting. But everyone talked about the classic confrontation: George Brett versus the Goose. "I think George was waiting for him," Leonard laughed. "He threw that fastball and it was all over. I was so nervous that when Gossage came in, I came in to the clubhouse here and watched it on TV. Dean Vogelaar was here, and I said, 'If U. L. Washington can get on base, George is gonna hit a home run.' And sure enough!" Leonard laughed. "I said, 'I can't believe it!' I never did anything like this before, forecasting things!"

George Brett's happiness bordered on dementia. Dripping with champagne, he clutched the stub of a bat handle in one hand, a champagne bottle in the other, and shouted for joy. "Oh, my God, what a feeling, Denny!" he told Royals play-by-play announcer Denny Matthews, standing by the clubhouse door. "You know, the biggest kick I got was seeing how *quiet* fifty-six thousand people could be!" He shrieked with laughter. "I never heard it so quiet here! It was great! It was great!" He looked around at the clubhouse in pandemonium. "I thought I'd been in tough situations before—trying to hit .400, the play-offs before, the fifth games, facing Guidry in the last game . . ." He shook his head. "That was *nothin*'! We knew we had to win tonight. . . . I've never felt anything like this, never before in my life!"

Brett tried to regain his breath. "I come in today, I don't know *what* to do. I had a great year, but I wasn't swinging the bat good in the play-offs. . . . Lau's got me figured out. . . . Guidry threw me all crud, some slow stuff, some sliders, some breaking balls, some change-ups . . . and he kinda messed with my mind a little bit. Then I thought Rudy May, who was a breaking-ball pitcher, would do the same thing. He threw me all fastballs! So I didn't know *what* to expect from Tommy John, and John was pitching me tough. So once I saw Rich Gossage coming in"—he beamed—"I was very relieved, 'cause I knew *exactly* what he was gonna do. He had one thing in mind. To blow it right by me. But I feel I'm a better fastball hitter than anything. I feel I can handle anybody's fastball. I've handled Nolan Ryan's and handled Gossage's before—but I haven't gotten many hits. When I went up there, Denny, the bat felt just like . . ." He held up the broken-off bat handle. "I think you should tell everybody what I'm holding—"

"Well," Matthews said, "you're holding about a three-inch stub."

"Yeah, of a bat. The bat felt really light . . ."

Just then, Reggie Jackson appeared at Brett's side, bearing a message of congratulations; and at the sight of Jackson—the slugger, the pull hitter, the symbol of the Yankees—something triggered in Brett's mind. "Hey," he cried, "I want everybody to know this. People in Kansas City got down on Charley!" Brett turned to Jackson. "Is he a hell of a guy?"

"Charley Lau is a hell of a guy," Jackson shouted, "he's a good man." He nodded. "I honestly think that I could hit forty home runs *without* Charley Lau—"

Brett interrupted. "But could you hit *.300* without Charley Lau?"

The Pitch

"—but Charley Lau will get you out of a rut *sooner*."
Jackson hesitated, distracted by the uproar in the locker
room. "George Brett is gonna hit and I'm gonna hit, but
Charley gets you out of your rut sooner and gives you
somebody to talk to and keep your mind right. *I* need
support and confidence," Jackson cocked his head at
Brett, "and even the best hitter in baseball—which
George Brett *is*—needs confidence too. . . ."

Back in Kansas City, celebrants clogged the streets of
Westport, stopped traffic in the Plaza, and partied at
Crown Center: shouting, laughing, hooting, singing,
honking horns. Thousands headed downtown with their
car radios on, the sounds of the Royals clubhouse
celebration crackling everywhere in the night. All too
soon the show would be over, the radio mikes put away
in New York, clubhouse hysterics giving way to a more
subdued exhilaration, a feeling of accomplishment.
There were still a few reporters present, though, when
George Brett turned at his locker with a grin on his face.
"I wish my dad were here now," he said, "he would have
really enjoyed this."

Acknowledgments

"They are a very robust family," a wire service reporter told me when I was just getting into this book. I found the Bretts to be that and more: spontaneous, unevasive, and candid—sometimes, brutally so. I owe them all for their time and cheerful cooperation, with special thanks to Jack Brett, who opened his scrapbook and his heart with the knowledge that these pages would inevitably subject him to uncomfortable scrutiny.

George and Bobby Brett reviewed the manuscript for factual accuracy (although they are in no way responsible for any error which may have slipped through); Pat Woodrum and Becky Chastain transcribed, typed, and assembled the manuscript with cheerful dispatch and an editorial eye; and Hank Young produced the photographs of George Brett during the drive for "four-zero-zero."

247

ACKNOWLEDGEMENTS

Thanks must go to the Royals public relations office—Dean Vogelaar, Bruce Carnahan, and Chris Stathos—for their help with the files, their assistance in contacting players, and for access to the musty scrapbooks in the code-a-phone room; to Bob Fromme and Ed O'Donnell of the Royals Baseball Network and WIBW radio, Topeka, for permission to quote from Royals broadcasts; and to the sportswriters and columnists of the *Kansas City Star* and *Times,* the AP and UPI, who were either quoted or interviewed for this book.

I am, of course, indebted to the editors of the various magazines under whose auspices I gathered much of the material for this book: Ellie Kossack, Berry Stainback, and John Devaney of *Sport* magazine; Robert Creamer and Larry Keith of *Sports Illustrated;* Rick Cerrone of *Baseball Magazine;* and Joyce Wagner of *City* magazine.

J.G.